T. Harrington, Timothy Charles Harrington

The Maamtrasna Massacre

Impeachment of the Trials

T. Harrington, Timothy Charles Harrington

The Maamtrasna Massacre
Impeachment of the Trials

ISBN/EAN: 9783743418790

Manufactured in Europe, USA, Canada, Australia, Japa

Cover: Foto ©ninafisch / pixelio.de

Manufactured and distributed by brebook publishing software (www.brebook.com)

T. Harrington, Timothy Charles Harrington

The Maamtrasna Massacre

THE MAAMTRASNA MASSACRE.

Impeachment of the Trials.

BY

T. HARRINGTON, M.P.

(With Appendix containing Report of Trials and Correspondence between Most Rev. Dr. M'Evilly and the Lord Lieutenant.)

DUBLIN:
NATION OFFICE,
70 MIDDLE ABBEY STREET.
1884.

INTRODUCTION

MAAMTRASNA, the scene of the barbarous murder, whose strange history is treated of in the following chapters, is situated in the County of Galway, at the head of a rugged glen, running up from one of the inlets of Lough Mask. On the night of August 17th, 1882, a party of men broke into a house in this village, occupied by a man named John Joyce, murdered him, his mother, wife, and a young daughter, and inflicted upon his two sons, the only other occupants of the house, injuries so severe, that one of them died on the following day, while the second lay for some time in a precarious condition.

Acting on the information of two brothers named Anthony and John Joyce, the police arrested, on the 20th, ten men, all of whom resided at a considerable distance from the scene of the murder—some at a distance of seven miles. The story related by those two brothers, supported by the son of one of them, was of so extraordinary a character that no one but the Crown officials seemed to credit it, and the suspicion very generally prevailed that the brothers Joyce had themselves more to do with the murder than the men they accused. However, after the customary remands and inquiries, the ten men were duly returned for trial at the Galway Assizes.

The " Prevention of Crimes Act " being in force at the time, the Crown availed of its provisions to have the venue changed to the City of Dublin, though there was no suggestion in the evidence of the witnesses, and nothing in the circumstances of the case to warrant the belief that the murder was of an agrarian character.

Some days previous to the trial, which commenced on 13th November, 1882, before a Special Jury of the City and County of Dublin, in Green Street Courthouse, it became known that Anthony Philbin, one of the accused, had become approver, and would be produced by the Crown to corroborate the three Joyces.

It is needless to say that such an announcement caused a complete change in the public feeling with regard to the story related by these witnesses, and everything in their evidence which had appeared absurd or incredible was forgotten in view of the declaration by one of the accused, that he was a participator in the horrible tragedy and could corroborate their testimony. On the first day of the trial another of the accused offered his services to the Crown and was accepted.

Portion of the revelations and arguments which the reader will meet with in these pages goes to prove that the first of the two approvers knew nothing of the murder, and was terrified into corroborating upon oath, a story which, even with regard to himself, was absolutely false; and that the second, Thomas Casey, though an actual participator in the murder, and willing as well as able to testify the truth, yet had no other means open to him to save his wretched life except by corroboration and perjury.

Applications on the part of prisoners' counsel for postponement, and for what is known as a "view jury," were refused. The juries were packed after the manner of all political and agrarian trials in Ireland. Eight minutes' deliberation sufficed to satisfy the mind and consciences of the first jury, and Patrick Joyce was adjudged guilty and sentenced to death. Patrick Casey was then immediately put upon his trial on the same evidence, and the jury gave 12 minutes' consideration to his fate. The learned judge, when passing sentence of death upon him, used the following words:—" But the "evidence has established clearly and conclusively, and "so as not to leave a doubt of your guilt upon the "mind of any sane person who has heard or read that "evidence, that you not only murdered Brigid Joyce, "but four other persons on that one occasion." No sooner was he cleared out of the dock than a third prisoner, Myles Joyce, was ushered in to be tried, on the same evidence, and before jurors who were in court listening to the judge's characterization of it.

Six minutes' retirement satisfied the jury, and his death also was decreed.

The fate of the three decided the issue for the remainder. Overtures were made to them to plead guilty on promise of escaping capital punishment. Some refused stoutly, and still protested they knew nothing of the murder. But their clergyman was called in, and he, by pointing out to them that if they were innocent their vindication might come in good time, induced them to accept the terms held out to them.

The next episode in the ghastly drama was the execution, at Galway Jail, of the three men who had been found guilty. A day or two before the execution two of the condemned sent, by direction of their spiritual adviser, for a magistrate, and made before him dying declarations, wherein each admitted his own guilt, and both protested that the third man, Myles Joyce, was innocent of the murder.

The Lord Lieutenant disregarded these declarations, and on the 15th December, 1882, the three men were brought forth together to execution. The scene was a painful and a shocking one. Two men walked calmly to their fate, but the third, Myles Joyce, turned to every official of the jail he met, as he passed to the scaffold, and, with all the fiery vehemence of the Celt, declared, in a language which nearly all those who surrounded him were strangers to, that "he was innocent. He feared not to die. But he felt the indignity of being put to death as a murderer." The scene on the scaffold itself was shocking beyond description. Even with the cap drawn over his eyes, and the executioner standing, rope in hand, to hurl the three wretched men together into eternity, Myles Joyce still declared his innocence ; and, as if eager that his very last breath on earth should be a protestation to that God whom he was so soon to meet, he turned again in the direction of the few bystanders, and "called God to witness that he knew no more of the murder than the child unborn ;" and with that solemn declaration on his lips he sunk from view. His last effort had somewhat displaced the arrangements of the executioner. The rope caught in the wretched man's arm, and for some seconds it was seen being jerked and tugged in the writhing of his last agony. The grim hangman cast an angry glance into the pit, and then, hissing an obscene oath at the struggling victim, sat on the beam, and kicked him into eternity.

It is needless to say that the publication of these harrowing particulars would, in themselves, have produced a sensation, but the fact which chiefly seized upon the public mind in Ireland was the declaration of innocence made by the man in his dying moments, and the public conscience already felt ill at ease as to the justice of the act that had been done.

At this time the fact that the other two men made dying declarations regarding him had not leaked out beyond the confines of the jail. Soon, however, the writer of these lines became aware of it, and asked a question upon the subject in the House of Commons. The reply of the Chief Secretary was evasive, beyond admitting that the depositions had been made. Again and again a question as to the contents of these documents was repeated in one form or another, but Mr. Trevelyan steadily refused to give any information, and the Prime Minister when finally appealed to only availed of the question as an occasion to pay a compliment to the "discretion and clemency with which he knew his noble friend Earl Spencer discharged his duties."

But yet the depositions which might be supposed to be the best testimony to the noble earl's discretion, &c., were denied to Parliament and the public. The denial of them strengthened suspicions already entertained, and gradually the feeling spread that Myles Joyce's death was a "judicial murder," and it was so characterised in Parliament by the present writer and others during the Session of 1883.

The witnesses who gave evidence for the Crown have been all living in the locality since the trial under the protection of police. In the month of July last it was noticed that Thomas Casey, one of the approvers, had presented himself at the confessional in the church of the parish to which he belongs, and the fact was of course regarded as significant, inasmuch as it was known that none of the other witnesses had ever presented themselves for Sacraments since the murder.

On the 8th August His Grace the Archbishop of Tuam visited the parish on his annual confirmation tour. Casey sought an interview with His Grace, and informed him of his desire to make reparation by a public confession for the double crime of murder and perjury committed by him in connection with the Maamtrasna trials. The revelations made by him before the archbishop, priests and congregation assembled in the church were immediately brought under the notice of Parliament, and a promise was extracted from the Marquis of Hartington that if they were brought officially before the Government by the Most Rev. Dr. M'Evilly an inquiry would be instituted.

Philbin, the other approver, reluctantly confessed to the truth of Casey's revelations.

His Grace, the Most Rev. Dr. M'Evilly brought the facts under the notice of the Lord Lieutenant, and requested an inquiry. Earl Spencer replied by a memorandum (to be found in the annexed Appendix), prepared evidently by the incriminated officials, and endeavouring to show that there were no grounds for suspicion, and no need of inquiry. This reply did not meet the case, and His Grace again pointed out the necessity for satisfying the public mind with an impartial inquiry.

To this communication Earl Spencer directed a curt refusal "to re-open the subject."

Such, briefly, is a history of the events which led to the preparation of the following chapters. If they do not obviate inquiry on the part of Earl Spencer or the Government, it is hoped at least they will help the public to see some of the ugly facts which an inquiry would serve to bring forth.

Owing to the frequent recurrence of the names Casey and Joyce, which are the names chiefly prevailing in the district, some confusion of persons will be inevitable to the cursory reader. Where, however, different persons possess the same Christian and surname a glance at the following list will be useful in distinguishing them :—

LIST OF NAMES.

ARRESTED FOR THE MURDER.

Patrick Joyce, Shanvallycahill,	executed, guilty
Patrick Casey,	executed, guilty
Myles Joyce,	executed, innocent
Michael Casey,	penal servitude, guilty
Martin Joyce (brother to Myles),	penal servitude, innocent
Patrick Joyce, Cappanacreha (another brother),	penal servitude, innocent
Tom Joyce (son of Patrick),	penal servitude, innocent
John Casey (little), Cappanacreha,	penal servitude, innocent
Anthony Philbin,	approver
Thomas Casey,	approver

THE ACTUAL MURDERERS (NOW ALLEGED).

John Casey (big), Bun-na-cnic,	supposed leader, at large
John Casey, Junr. (his son), Bun-na-cnic,	at large
Pat Joyce, Shanvallycahill	executed
Pat Casey,	executed
Pat Leyden,	now in England
Michael Casey,	penal servitude
Thomas Casey,	approver

INDEPENDENT WITNESSES.

Anthony Joyce
John Joyce, Derry (his brother)
Patrick Joyce, Derry (John's son)

OTHERS.

John Joyce, Maamtrasna,	the murdered man
Michael Joyce (boy), do. (son),	who died of wounds
Patrick Joyce (boy), do. (son),	who recovered

John Joyce (young), Bun-na-cnic, the man whom the murderers called out to join them

THE
MAAMTRASNA MURDERS.

THE APPROVER CASEY'S REVELATIONS ABOUT THE CROWN OFFICIALS.

CHAPTER I.

Visit to the Scene of the Murder.

The revelations recently made by the informer, Thomas Casey, in connection with the horrible massacre at Maamtrasna, form but one, and by no means the strangest chapter, in the extraordinary history of this crime and its punishment. The wholesale character of the murder, the want of any sufficient motive to account for the crime, the singularly strange story of the men who alleged that they tracked the murderers for miles and witnessed the horrible tragedy, the trials, the dying protestations, the reticence of Government with regard to some facts, and their unwonted readiness to defend themselves by the publication of others, the plea of guilty made in the dock by men believed to be innocent, the confession of one man that though wholly ignorant of even the slightest knowledge of the murder, he swore himself guilty that he might save his own life by the sacrifice of others, and the allegation that the real murderers are at large, and known to the Crown, while men of whose innocence it is assured, lie in jail—all combine to form a story that might well challenge the pen of the most sensational novelist of our time.

The duty to which I have devoted a few days among the peasantry in this wild region was not undertaken for the purpose of catering to the taste of the curious and sensational. My purpose was to unravel to some extent the mystery in which this story is enveloped, and to strengthen the position of those who demand that justice shall be done. With this view I have carefully studied the history of the case, have travelled over the ground, measured certain distances, and sketched objects of importance referred to in evidence. I have also held repeated interviews with the families of the imprisoned men, with the informers and their families, and even conversed with the two men whom Thomas Casey states planned and paid for the murder. It is only by such an examination as this, and with a copy of the evidence given at the trials in a man's hand, that he can properly understand the force of the statements that have been recently made by the informers Casey and Philbin. Keen as is the interest which these statements have created throughout Ireland, it yet but faintly reflects the feeling of burning anxiety aroused among the peasantry in this rugged glen.

THE POPULAR BELIEF

not alone among the people of the locality, but everywhere I have travelled in the surrounding country, is confident and unshaken as to the complete innocence of Myles Joyce, who was executed, and his brothers, Martin and Pat, who are in penal servitude, as well as Pat's son Thomas, and John Casey, who are also in penal servitude. Indeed in this respect at least the confession of Thomas Casey was no revelation to the people of Maamtrasna and Cappanacreha. Local gossip has long ago threshed out every feature of the case which presents itself to their untutored minds, and evidence of the very strongest character has come under my notice to convince me that long even before the Crown had proved its case the women had got into one another's confidence during their visits to Cong and Galway and Dublin in connection with their husbands' defence, and no doubt remained with them, at least as to the men who were out of their beds on the fatal night, and the men who were not. Belief in the innocence of these men is by no means confined to the populace. In the course of my investigation I had many opportunities of meeting the police who are a long time resident in the locality scattered over the glen in barracks, huts, and protection posts, and wherever I had an opportunity of getting into confidential relations with a member of the force I found him to share fully the popular belief as to the guilty and the innocent. It is no exaggeration to say that there is not a peasant in the district—and scarcely a policeman—(who, by the way, are almost as numerous here as the peasantry) that attaches the slightest credence to the evidence of the three Joyces, the so-called independent witnesses. Everyone can repeat the story of the manner in which Anthony Joyce, whose brain is believed to have conceived the "independent evidence," learned with surprise of the murder of his cousin John the next day from a little girl, his daughter, who came to the bog where he was working with several more of his neighbours, and there is no man in the district more anxious to emphasise this fact than Anthony's own brother, Michael Joyce. They point, at the same time to the fact that before Anthony put his strange story into shape he first took care to go to the house of the murdered family, and by inspection assure himself that there should be no circumstance in the number of bullet wounds, or the position of affairs generally, that could give contradiction to his story; and, having so far satisfied himself, he summoned a small family council in his brother John's house, to which only John, his son and daughter were invited, and then Anthony sought the police.

Before entering into details, as I shall have to do pretty fully in the following, it may be convenient to state down here in general terms what are

THE RESULTS OF MY INQUIRY.

In the first place, I hope to be able to show that the tale which the three Joyces related as to their having tracked the murderers was not only doubtful and incredible, but impossible; that each of their statements is contradictory; and the whole three at variance with one another. I shall show that Philbin, the informer, so far from being, as he swore, present at the murder, did not even know the locality, and that his evidence discredits rather than corroborates the Joyces, while the original evidence of Thomas Casey differs from all in many points of striking importance. I hope also to satisfy my readers as to the motives which prompted the murderers as well as the motives which influenced Anthony Joyce and his brother in wrongfully accusing his three cousins, Myles, Martin and Pat, and the manner in which Anthony was able to bring a grain of truth into his story, by having four guilty men among the ten whom he charged. Furthermore, I am in a position to show—and I make no light estimate of the gravity of the charge, and the difficulties which may lie in the way of its proof—that the authorities had in their possession at the time of the trial evidence which would have completely proved the story of the Joyces to be a fabrication, and that they chose to suppress this evidence rather than discredit the testimony of those so-called independent witnesses. And now, when the truth is forced upon them, they suffer the actual murderers to remain at large, within half a mile of the scene of the massacre, rather than discredit their former proceedings by a new trial. My inquiries have also resulted in a full corroboration in every essential detail of the story unfolded by Thomas Casey in his recent revelations, and given by him to me in a manner much more minute and circumstantial than it has yet appeared.

The difficulties which have to be overcome in pursuing inquiry into this extraordinary case are by no means slight. To those presented by the locality, and the almost impassible mountain track upon which the traveller has to trust himself to the instinct of his sure-footed pony, are to be added the extreme reluctance of the people to give any information in view of possible and very probable prosecutions against some of their near neighbours or relatives, and the fact that English is almost completely unknown among them, and any attempt at seeking information except through the medium of their mother tongue must end in failure.

On the first occasion of my visit to the district, I was accompanied by Rev. J. Corbet, P.P., Partry, and his curate, Rev. J. M'Donnell. Glensaul, where the two approvers, Thomas Casey and Anthony Philbin reside, is in the parish of Partry, or, more correctly speaking, Toomakeady ; but Maamtrasna, as well as Derry, Cappanacreha, and Shanvallycahill, are portion of the extensive parish of Ross, whose P.P. is the Rev. Father Mellet, of Clonbur. Neither of my reverend companions had ever before been in the district where the murder was committed. But I could soon see that the fame of the rev. Pastor of Partry had preceded him, that they were not unacquainted with the strong bond of sympathy between him and his people, while his skill in the use of their mother tongue made them quite at ease. Even my own very imperfect knowledge of it, which enabled me with some difficulty to hold converse with them, was, next to the introduction by the *soggart*, the surest passport which I could possess ; and, though my sins against syntactical law must have been manifold and grievous, and occasionally excited their laughter, I yet found they had not the same dread of my open note book that they would have in the case of a more un-Irish " special."

PROTESTATIONS OF INNOCENCE.

In a public letter upon this case I had occasion to refer to the dying declarations of the two men Pat Joyce and Pat Casey, who were executed with Myles Joyce. I may mention in passing, that this man Pat Joyce was not a relative of Myles. The recent official memorandum (see Appendix) of the Under-Secretary, as well as the answers of Mr. Trevelyan in Parliament, purported to draw attention to some vagueness in the declarations in which these men asserted the innocence of Myles Joyce. Facts which have since come to my knowledge show up in a very unpleasant light this trick on the part of the Castle officials. Both men were purley Irish-speaking peasants, and the attempt to discredit their dying declarations upon the ground of vagueness, is as disgraceful a sham as Castle government in Ireland ever attempted. I am furthermore assured that, so far from being vague, their declarations distinctly state the innocence, not alone of Myles Joyce, but of the other four men now in penal servitude, and corroborate to the full Casey's statements of the number of persons who were present at the murder. If that be so, a very ready explanation is afforded of the reluctance of Earl Spencer to produce these depositions. From an official source of undoubted veracity, I learned, before I visited Maamtrasna, that four men in penal servitude, whose innocence Casey recently deposed to, have, from the very day of their reprieve, declared in the most emphatic language their entire innocence of any complicity in the murder, while the fifth man has never concealed his guilt, as I shall show later on.

This fact received striking corroboration from inquiries which we made immediately on our visit to the place. We found that long before Casey made his revelations these four men, ignorant of all that was passing in the world outside, invariably referred in their letters home to their unjust incarceration. I append a few specimens of their letters. Their simple, artless style will tell more eloquently than any words of mine could with sympathetic readers. As early as June, 1883, John Casey thus wrote to his wife:—

"Her Majesty's Convict Prison,
"Mountjoy, Dublin, 15th June, 1883.

"DEAR MARY—I received your welcome letter after I came to this prison. I was very happy to find you and children and friends were all right well. I am very well myself, thank God. I am going to school every day, and to chapel every day. We have Mass three times a week. I have nothing to complain of; everything is very cleane. I have flannels and a good bed and good cloths; write whin you get this, and let me know how my mother is, and my brother my sister and her family, your father and mother, and brothers, and did you here from your sister; also let me know how Michael Connboy and his family, and your old uncle Pat, or is he alive yet; also Napy Liden. *Dear Mary, it is very hard to be here for a crime that I know nothing about. Thanks be to God I know nothing whatever about it. But I fret more for you and the children then I do for myself, for you know as well as I do myself, that I had no hand in that act. You need not fret, for God is good, and we will all be happy yet with the help of God.* Let me know when you write have you any pigs, how the crops are, and did you pay the rint yet, *and I hope you and I will be happy together yet, with the help of God* No more at present from your loving husband,

"JOHN CASEY.

"To Mary Casey,"

Twelve months later he wrote :—

"Mountjoy, Dublin, 27, 6, '84.

"MY DEAR WIFE—It gave me great pleasure to learn from your last letter that you were all well. I am in very good health, thank God. I have every convenience.

"When writing let me know how is my mother, and brother, my sister and family, and your own father and mother also, and brothers. Let me know did your sister send for Thomas. Let me know how is Michael Conboy and family. I wish to know do your uncle Patrick and wife live Let me know how is Napy Lyden. I hope you and the priest will petition the Lord Lieutenant as quickly as possible. *It is very hard for me to have been in prison and separated from my family, especially as I am innocent.* Let me know are the crops promising this year. You wished to know in the last letter had I been working hard, and also used I get tobacco. I have not been working hard. As for getting tobacco that is contrary to the rules I wish to know did Peter get married. I hope he and father will mind the children in my absence. I hope that will not be very long. Keep good courage and I will do the same. *I hope everything will come to light hereafter. I don't expect to be always here.*

"No more at present, and remain, with fond love,

"JOHN CASEY.

"Mary Casey."

Martin Joyce (brother to Myles Joyce, who was executed, and Pat Joyce, who is also in jail) wrote as follows to his wife a week before our visit :—

".Mountjoy Prison, 5th Sept., 1884.

"MY DEAR WIFE—I am very happy to inform you that I am in the enjoyment of excellent health, thank God. I hope yourself and the children are enjoying the same blessing. When you write send me all the news of yourself and the children, and how you all are getting along, your mother in particular. I hope she is strong and in good health ; Bridget Lyons and her children, also my brother Anthony and his family, and John Casey's family. I hope they are well. John is in good health himself here. Let me know also when you write how is John Duffy and his wife, Michael Casey and his wife and family. I hope they are all well. Give my blessing to Mrs. Casey.

"*I hope that God in his just mercy, who saved me from death, will yet show to the world my innocence of any participation in the crime for which I am the innocent sufferer.* My dear wife, I also wish to let you know that my brother Pat has been removed to Maryborough prison about a week ago. He was sent there for his own good, through the kindness of the doctor, for he wasn't sick, only a little lonely for leaving us here behind him. It is about 50 miles from here, and a fine healthy place. Don't forget to mention when you write how the crops are, and how you are advanced with the harvest. Write as soon as you can.—Your affectionate husband,

"MARTIN JOYCE."

CHAPTER II.

THE CASE FOR THE CROWN.

BEFORE touching upon what I believe will be found the true history of the Maamtrasna massacre, or calling in the aid of any revelations recently made by the approvers, it is well, first of all, to examine the case as it was presented by the Crown at the trial, and to see how much may be gathered from it to favour the theory as to the innocence of some of the accused. The memorandum published by the Under-Secretary some time since, in reply to His Grace the Archbishop of Tuam, sought to discredit the revelations of the approvers, Casey and Philbin, upon the ground that both men were desirous to get back into favour with the people among whom they live. If the Crown is justified in assuming that a sufficient reason to doubt their confessions, I think I may safely take it that what they themselves style " a desire to save their necks " would furnish sufficient motive to them to lie in their original evidence.

RELATIONS BETWEEN ACCUSED AND ACCUSERS.

For the present, therefore, we may leave out of consideration their testimony at the trial, and confine ourselves to the three Joyces, called by courtesy "independent witnesses." That these men lived in perpetual feud with the accused is beyond all question. Myles Joyce, who was executed, lived within two hundred yards of Anthony Joyce, while Pat Joyce and his son Thomas, at present in penal servitude, resided still nearer. Their little holdings are mixed in and out among one another, and the rough slight little stone fences that divide them here and there afforded ample opportunity for quarrel by the trespass of the cattle of one on the farm of the other. But the main cause of their quarrels—the same cause that has led to many a crime in the district, and that will be found to be at the bottom both of this barbarous murder in the first instance, and the judicial murder in the second—arose from the intermingling of their sheep on the mountain pasture, held by them in common, and the ready means which it afforded to any man to help himself to the sheep of his neighbour. For a period of thirteen years preceding the trial Anthony Joyce and Myles Joyce had spoken to one another only in quarrel; and a very short time before the murder at Maamtrasna Myles got a month's imprisonment in Galway Jail from Anthony for assault arising out of one of these disputes. They fought on the *boreen* between their houses, and though Myles Joyce bore from his neighbours the best character of any man in the locality, Anthony knew the trick of the law too well for him, and succeeded in imprisoning him.

One circumstance in their relations with one another is worthy of note as illustrating the characters of both men. A child of Anthony Joyce's died, and Myles, for the first time in many years, went to Anthony's house to the wake. Some time later it happened that a similar affliction befel Myles himself. Anthony was obdurate in his enmity, and never went near Myles' house to show his sympathy. With Pat Joyce, Myles' brother, who is now in penal servitude, Anthony carried on perpetual war. They were at law with one another for trespass and assault almost every other month, and on one occasion, when returning at night from the court, Pat was severely beaten by men whom Anthony is accused of having employed for the purpose. Martin, the second brother of Myles Joyce, who is now in prison, besides his sympathy with his brothers, had a quarrel on his own account with Anthony and his brother John, and was accused by them of having drowned in the lake a mare and foal belonging to John, the second of the independent witnesses. Pat Joyce, of Shanvalleycahill, was accused by them of being concerned in this transaction also; while the Caseys, who were John Joyce's immediate neighbours, were always engaged in the same quarrels with him that the other Joyces waged with the brother Anthony.

Now, even assuming that the immense sums of money which these two brothers received from the Crown did not warp their " independence " or the honesty of their evidence, have we not at least in the circumstances above related good grounds for treating their accusation against these men with suspicion ? These facts cannot be disputed. When it suited the purpose of the Crown they were freely proclaimed. In endeavouring to account for the extraordinary story of Anthony Joyce about pursuing the men for miles at night, the Attorney-General, now Mr. Justice Johnson, said at the trial :—

"There was reason why Anthony Joyce thought it necessary to keep an eye upon the party, and they (the jury) would see that from a cross-examination by the prisoner at the bar (Pat Joyce), because before the magistrates he asked John Joyce had he not a spite against him, and he replied that there was not an outrage in the country that he was not at the head of, and that he should have been hanged years ago."

THE INDEPENDENT TESTIMONY.

To enable my readers to follow the observations I shall have to make upon the evidence of the Joyces, as well as to grasp the state of the case before Casey and Philbin became approvers, it will be necessary for me to quote in full the evidence of one of these witnesses. I shall take that of Anthony Joyce, for beyond all question to him belongs the credit of laying the plot of the case for the Crown. I quote from the *Freeman* report of the trial of Pat Joyce, of Shanvallycahill :—

"Anthony Joyce was examined through the interpreter by Mr. Murphy—He recollected the night of the 17th August. He was not sure at what hour he went to bed that night. When he had been in bed some time the barking of his dogs awoke him. He got up and went to the door, and saw six men, whom he did not know at first. He then went round to the back of his house and he saw the six men again there. He then recognised the six men. Their names were—Anthony Philbin, Tom Casey, Martin Joyce, Myles Joyce, Patrick Joyce, and Tom Joyce, of Cappanacreha. He had known four of the men since his youth, but two of them lived some distance away from him, Tom Casey and Anthony Philbin. Witness after a time went to the house of his brother, having nothing on him but his shirt, trousers, and a flannel vest. He went the ' short cut,' his brother and nephew came out. He then observed the six men going to the house of Michael Casey. Witness and his brother and nephew followed them. They went into Casey's house, and on coming out they went the back road. The number of men at this time was ten. The other four were Pat Joyce (Shanvallycahill), Patrick Casey, John Casey, and Michael Casey. Witness saw them coming out of a house and went behind a hedge. Witness went down after them, accompanied by his brother and nephew. The ten men then went towards the lake until they came to the river Strangalaun, when they crossed the river and went towards Maamtrasna. Witness and his companions were following them, no matter where they might go. He knew John Joyce's house at Maamtrasna. He saw the ten men go up to that house, and then he heard a noise at the door. At this time witness, his brother, and nephew were behind a bush. Some of the ten men went in and others remained outside. Witness heard noise like people beating at the door. He heard people in the house shouting and screeching. He could not distinguish the screams of women from those of men. He did not wait after that, but he and his brother and nephew ran back as quickly as they could to their own houses. Witness stayed with his brother from that time until the break of day. He saw the police next day about dinner time. On Saturday he was at Finny, and saw some of the men taken by the police."

Even to a person who has never seen the locality this extraordinary story presents difficulties amounting to incredulity, and everyone who remembers the time when the Joyces first made their tale public knows that it was laughed at as absurd until the corroboration of the informers; but it is only upon a minute examination of the route described and the other circumstances detailed in the evidence that the audacity of its concoction can be properly appreciated. One fact necessary to be kept in mind through the whole examination of these men's evidence is that the night of the murder was quite dark. Reference to the calendar would prove this, but the Attorney-General in his statement of the case admitted that " the new moon was about her fourth day, and therefore there was not much light." The distance which they alleged they travelled that night, creeping stealthily, three men in pursuit of ten, whose purpose they allege they did not know, is three miles at the very least computation. From the evidence, one would naturally assume that alleged pursuit took place along a fairly level road. So far from this being the case, there is not scarcely in all the mountain districts of Ireland a path more difficult to travel either by day or night. Under no circumstances could two men walk abreast along one hundred yards of it. Running along the mountain side, parallel to the shore of the lake, and about midways between it and the summit of the mountain this path forms the boundary between the cultivated patches and the barren mountain slieve. On the lower side it is defined by a low fence guarding the cultivated patches, but on the right or mountain side there is for the most part no fence except here and there—the sides of the rocks by which it leads. Deep mountain ravines with small streams cut it at various intervals, and at those places loose rolling stones cover the track and would be likely to reveal the pursuer at a much greater distance than his vision could reach on a dark night. Such is the character of the road by which Anthony Joyce and his brother and nephew followed, as they allege, barefooted, a party of ten men at dead of a dark night through the mere curiosity of learning what they meant to do. Now, Anthony Joyce's house is situated 47 feet from the road, on the left side, as one proceeds by the track he alleged to have been taken by the accused. The house is built at right angles to the road, or boreen, with the door facing eastward, but a barn built from the end of the house runs in front, parallel to the road, rendering it impossible to obtain a view of the road at any nearer distance than 80 or 100 yards from the door, and here it only commands a view of 4 or 5 yards in length. Anthony Joyce could only see the road from his open door, for there is no window in the house affording a view of the road. To credit this portion of his story we should believe that on a very dark night he could discern six men against the black mountain background, at a distance of 80 or 100 yards. He was awakened from sleep, he says, by his dogs barking. What became of the dogs when he opened the door and looked out? Does any one believe they would not have run at the passers-by, or, at least, so alarmed them as to attract attention to his opening the door as the men approached it? Had these men such a feeling of perfect security passing the house of their greatest enemy, that neither the barking of his dogs nor the opening of his door attracted their observation? Now, two out of the six men lived nearer to the scene of the murder than Anthony Joyce. They were the two men, Pat and Tom Joyce, father and son, who are now in prison. What could have brought them past his house? If they were to join a murderous expedition on that night, does any one believe they would not have gone direct to the alleged place of rendezvous, instead of parading backwards and forwards before the house of their greatest living enemy, Anthony Joyce? The recognition, he says, took place back of his house. If he dressed himself even partially, as he describes, before going back of the house, the men must have been too far gone to recognise them. If, on the other hand, this partial dressing took place after recognising them, then his theory that he reached his brother's house before them is impossible. Upon either of these grounds Joyce's story must break down, and no jury having an opportunity of examining the place would ever have given it a moment's consideration.

Again, let us take another point in his evidence. He went to the house of his brother, he says, and knocked and woke him in sufficient time to show him the men approaching Michael Casey's house. Now, such a thing as a "short cut" is out of the question. The boreen is the most direct path between the houses, save that as both are to the left of the road a man might cut the fields parallel to the boreen. But surely the boreen would be an easier course to take than jumping over the fences that intervene, and exposing a man "wearing a white flannel vest" to the danger of being seen. John Joyce's house is about 400 yards distant from Anthony's, and Michael Casey's is just almost in a line with John Joyce's, but a few yards farther on. The view which all three Joyces say they got of the men entering Michael Casey's house at this point is simply impossible. Even in the broad day light Casey's house is not visible from John Joyce's, for a large barn and a double fence lined with trees shade Joyce's house from view of the road and of Casey's house, which is nearer the road.

The distance of John Joyce's house from the road by the most direct line is 122 yards, and no human eye could discern figures against the dark background of the mountain on such a night as we have described. I tried the experiment on one of the brightest days we have enjoyed this year, by asking one of the police who stood watching my movements as I sketched John Joyce's house whether he could tell me which of the constables was standing on the road facing us ? After considerable hesitation, he said " he thought it was Constable Murphy, for he was the stoutest of the four men in the hut." Now, Casey's house, where the Joyces allege they saw the six men entering, is farther away. It can scarcely be less than 200 yards, and yet John Joyce swore that on the dark night in question he was so well able to see six men at that distance that, though he did not then know them, he did recognise them among ten who afterwards came out of the house, while in the same breath he swore that the whole ten men wore dark clothes, and would give no more definite description of the dress of any of them. This is a sample of the independent testimony upon which the authorities now rely to discredit the confessions of Casey and Philbin. Almost at every point of their evidence the same difficulty presents itself. They were studiously and cleverly vague and indefinite in all they deposed to ; but yet, wherever they were reduced to particulars, their story becomes impossible.

In order to give themselves an opportunity of recognising the ten men, they bring themselves back of Michael Casey's house, waiting for them while they were in. Now back of Michael Casey's house means nearer to Maamtrasna, the scene of the massacre. Why should those three men go back of Michael Casey's house to watch ? They could not see the door from the position they allege they occupied. The men who went in could come out of Casey's house and go back again to Anthony Joyce's house without being observed by the three waiting seven yards behind the house which, from there, is concealed by a thick row of trees. They could not swear they believed the six men to be going to Maamtrasna. Why wait at all for them while they were in Michael Casey's house ? And, if they did wait, why assume the men would go on to Maamtrasna instead of returning to their homes ?

I shall show later on how strangely Philbin's evidence clashes with the Joyces at this point. Equally incredible is the story of the Joyces at every material point of the case. They alleged they took a "short cut" after leaving the school at Derry, and crossed to Maamtrasna to the house of the murdered man. Why should they assume that the ten men intended to go to that house ? Then, again, strangest of all, why not go to the police barrack so near the scene of the murder, and call in the assistance of the police ?

Why not take the men red-handed after the murder if it was not possible to seize them in time to prevent it? The car road to Finny police-station was the easiest, the shortest, and the safest mode of retreat open to those men who allege they were frightened, but yet they never sought the police. But the strangest fact of all, perhaps, is this—that the house of the murdered family was in the middle of a row of some ten houses, extending along the path or "street," as one of the witnesses called it, and these houses are nearly all occupied by Joyces and O'Briens, cousins of the murdered man and his wife. Anthony Joyce, himself, was a cousin of the murdered man. Yet his story is that he and his brother and nephew stood looking on at this cold-blooded massacre of his first cousin, while John (Mary) Joyce, Michael (Mary) Joyce, Michael (Pat) Joyce, Thomas O'Brien, and Michael O'Brien, all relatives of the murdered family, lived within a hundred yards or so of the house, and he never called them to stay the hand of the assassins. When I, in company with my reverend friends, called at Anthony's house on the first day of our visit to the glen, we were immediately struck with the reluctance he and his brother exhibited in coming to speak to us. A man with an honest story would scarcely have striven to avoid examination of it. Their attitude in this respect contrasted very much with that of Thomas Casey. But the conduct of the women was most remarkable. Both Anthony's wife and John's wife were most careful to avoid any corroboration of the story of their husbands. Women under such circumstances have a repugnance of telling a lie to the priest, and they always met our query as to whether they heard the husband get up or knew he was out by—"Indeed, I don't know anything about it. Ask him. He says he knows it all." Anthony did very grudgingly answer a few questions, but as I held his evidence in my hand, and reminded my reverend friend of a discrepancy, Father Corbett said—"That is not what you swore in Dublin!" Anthony replied, in very ungracious accents, "Well, whatever I swore in Dublin, I'll swear again. You are trying to make an angel in heaven of Casey, but did he not swear he was at the murder, and sure some of them admitted they were guilty."

I could not avoid the reflection that this was the voice of a man engaged in a hopeless controversy with his conscience to convince it that bringing justice upon the heads of a few guilty atoned for perjury and the sacrifice of some who were innocent.

CHAPTER III.

THE CROWN CASE—CONTINUED.

HAVING entered somewhat minutely into the evidence offered at the trial by Anthony Joyce, the principal of the so-called "independent witnesses," it will not be necessary to weary my readers with so detailed an examination of the evidence of his brother and nephew. If their strange tale were true, we should naturally expect to find them in agreement upon at least the main points of the case; and if, as I allege and hope to convince my readers, their evidence was from beginning to end pure fabrication, then also they should take care to make their statements agree in the main, and the story had been repeated by each of them six times in presence of the magistrates before they came to the edition which I have to deal with—viz., the evidence at the trial.

The most striking feature of agreement, however, which we meet in their statements is the vagueness with which every point of the story is related. It is difficult to refrain from admiring the skill with which they deal in generalities and the manner in which they avoid the specific statement of any particulars that might involve disagreement or contradiction.

Neither of them would say what hour at night they turned out; which of the men passed them first or last at the alleged point of recognition; what description of clothes any particular man wore; what man entered the house of the murder and what man did not; how many shots were fired; what description of arms the accused carried, nor any word they heard them speak to one another. Necessarily, however, they were drawn into an occasional particular here and there by cross-examination, and as the replies to these questions did not form part of the original plot, the approvers Casey and Philbin, who had not the advantage of hearing these few particulars related for them six times before the magistrates, make sad havoc when they came to offer their " corroboration:"

Here is a brief extract, worthy of special note, from the evidence of John Joyce, the brother of Anthony:—

"All my family were in bed. Anthony woke me, and I went out with him. I saw six persons near my house, but did not know them. I saw them go into Michael Casey's house, which is not far from mine. When they came out from Casey's house there were ten men in the party. I then knew them all. *When they came out of Casey's house I was able to recognise the six who had formed the first party.*"

Now, I have already pointed out the distance of Michael Casey's house from John Joyce's. Even assuming that Joyce came out and stood on the high ground between his house and Casey's, the men would still be nearly two hundred yards from him. There can be no doubt this is the nearest distance his tale would admit of, for he says in cross-examination afterwards, that the men were in Casey's while he was crossing the intervening field. How, in the name of common sense, could any man—even a Dublin special juror—be induced to believe that on this very dark night in question John Joyce was so well able to see the six men who entered a house two hundred yards away that he recognized them among ten who some time subsequently came out of the house? Just let anyone consider how long it would take him to mark six men walking together at that distance in the broad daylight so minutely as to know them among ten afterwards, and then he will have some idea how easy the task would be on a dark night, when even a close look into a man's face is necessary for recognition. But perhaps a very marked distinction in their dress—some bright dazzling colour that dispels 200 yards of darkness—lent its aid on the occasion. Unfortunately John Joyce gives evidence against himself here, for the following passage occurs in his subsequent cross-examination :—

"Could you describe the dresss of any of the men? I could not tell you how any of them were dressed. *They all wore dark clothes*"

If there were no other point in this man's testimony to render it unworthy of credit, this in itself would be sufficient. But everywhere it is equally absurd and incredible. His dogs, for example, are made to act in strange contrast to Anthony's dogs, and, indeed, to dogs in general. Anthony's sagacious brutes woke him up out of bed before the men had appeared at all in view of his house, and he was just at the door prepared for observation at the identical moment the six men were passing the five or six yards of the boreen which the view from the door commands. But John's dogs, knowing well the conduct that was required of them, at a later stage of the plot, never barked at all when Anthony came to their door at dead of night to wake up John and his boy Pat, and tell them his mysterious story about the six men on the road. "I opened the door at once," says truthful John Joyce. "I have dogs, but they did not bark." Of course, if these dogs barked they would have aroused the suspicion of the men alleged to be entering Casey's house, and so they discreetly held their tongues.

But I shall not dwell upon petty details of this kind. I know how uninteresting they must be to the general reader, and the revelations I shall have to make before I close my observations will render too minute an examination of this class of evidence unnecessary. It is well, however, to keep in mind the fact that these were the links of the chain of evidence upon which one innocent man was consigned to a murderer's grave, and four innocent men still lie suffering in jail. The only other independent witnesses relied upon by the Crown are Pat Joyce and Mary Joyce, the children of John. Mary is the only one of the women of the families that came forward to sustain the plot of the Joyces. Anthony's wife and children seem to have slept in security while he was away five or six hours, at dead of night, on his alleged expedition in pursuit of evidence, and John's wife and daughter Kate, also slept tranquilly. "How do you account for Mary Joyce coming forward to give evidence?" I said to a man living in the neighbourhood of the Joyces. "She never came forward, sir," he said, "until some weeks after the father and uncle gave evidence, and only then because it was reported that her father and Anthony were to be taken themselves for the murder. Everyone said they would have been put on their trial, as no one believed their story." This fact I got full corroboration of later on.

Mary's evidence, stated briefly, is this :—That she heard her uncle coming to the house and calling her father and brother out of bed, and telling them about the six men, and that she remained awake until their return. What strange conduct on the part of this girl not to have called up the other members of the family, nor even to take the trouble to look out and see what happened the father and brother and uncle during the four or five hours of the night that they must have been absent. Neither Mary, the father, nor brother would approach me or my reverend companion on the occasion of our visit to their house. They were at work in a field close by, their police escort basking lazily in the warm sun near the fence, and, though sent for by the other members of the family, they refused to come. Like Anthony's wife, Mrs. John declined to commit herself to any statement. "She knew nothing about it." The following extract from the dialogue between herself and my reverend companion is, however, very instructive :—

"Surely you know whether Anthony Joyce came to your house that night ?"

"Indeed I don't know anything about the case. Ask himself."

"Were you not sleeping with your husband ? You should hear him if he came to the house and called your husband ?"

"I was sleeping with him. Why not I hear the voice ?"

"Did you hear it ?"

"Why not I hear it ?"

"Did any of your children hear it ?"

"I don't know, indeed. There is always heavy sleep on young people ?"

Nothing could be more clear than this woman's desire to evade telling a direct lie, and at the same time to guard against our getting from the younger members of the family any information that would condemn her husband.

One extraordinary feature of the story told by these Joyces seems to have altogether escaped observation at the trial. In their evidence they all allege that they left the scene of the murder when they heard the screaming in the house. The family thus attacked at night were cousins of theirs. Yet they never came next morning, nor sent to inquire whether any murder had actually been committed amongst them, or find out how many, and who had been murdered.

IMPORTANT REVELATION.

But it would not be just to those who follow the history of this extraordinary case to waste a long time in pointing to inconsistencies and absurdities in the evidence of those men, while the relation of one important fact which I discovered in the course of my investigation completely and for ever sets the brand of perjury and falsehood upon their tale. Nice distinctions as to distances, minute examination of circumstances, contrasts and comparisons, may all be dismissed from consideration when I announce to my readers that beyond all question of doubt the men who murdered John Joyce and his family were disguised, had blackened faces, and wore white flannel vests, called among the peasantry of the West *bawneens*. One may well startle at being asked to believe that perjury so deliberate, so manifest, so diabolical in its conception and destructive in its effects would be committed by men of the class of Anthony and John Joyce. But what will my readers say when I ask them to believe that responsible officials of the Crown knew of this perjury and connived at it by suppressing the fact which I have now brought to light for the first time? Here is a crux for my Lord Spencer and his co-administrators in Dublin Castle. What now becomes of the famous memorandum in reply to his Grace the Archbishop of Tuam? If Earl Spencer cares to verify the fact, if he has any desire to bring peace to the official conscience for the death of Myles Joyce, let him pay a visit to Artane Industrial School and talk to the intelligent young child, Patrick Joyce, who was left for dead by the murderers; or let him go and consult the police of the locality to whom this boy and the elder brother who succumbed to his wounds gave this important information on the morning after the murder.

Why was it not followed up? Why were not the guilty pursued? Did it make no difference to the Crown officials whether their victim were guilty or innocent provided a holocaust of some kind were offered? Earl Spencer may refuse inquiry; he may not deem the life of a Connemara peasant and the lifelong liberty of a few others of sufficient importance to put his official satellites to the trouble of an inquiry. But it is beyond his power and theirs now to conceal the truth any longer, and the issue shall be inquiry, or confession of guilt. In a future chapter I shall describe the manner in which I came to learn and verify the important fact above mentioned, but that there may be no justification or defence for the conduct of Crown officials, I shall first have some criticisms to offer upon the evidence of the two approvers.

CHAPTER IV.

THE EVIDENCE OF THE APPROVERS AT THE TRIAL.

In the letter of the Under-Secretary to his Grace the Archbishop of Tuam, he states that:—

"There was ample evidence at the trial given by three unimpeached and independent witnesses to convict all the prisoners without the evidence of Thomas Casey or Anthony Philbin, and their recent statements do not shake that testimony, which plainly established that Myles Joyce and the prisoners now undergoing penal servitude were themselves members of that party who participated in, or actually committed, the murders of the Joyce family."

Few, I think, who have taken pains to follow the observations I have made up to the present with regard to this branch of the evidence will be disposed to agree with the view of the Under-Secretary. That the brothers Anthony and John Joyce and John's son were not unimpeachable or independent witnesses—that their evidence was not sufficient to bring guilt to any of the accused; in fact, that from beginning to end it was perjury of the blackest dye, I have, I think, fully and clearly established. But I propose to go farther, and to show that the evidence of these so-called "unimpeached witnesses," and the evidence of the informers combined, did not furnish grounds sufficient to deprive any man of his liberty, much less of his life. With this view I propose to offer a few criticisms upon the evidence given at the trial by

THE INFORMERS.

My contention simply is this—that Philbin, the first of the informers, was not at the scene of the murder and knew nothing of it; and that Thomas Casey, the other approver, though guilty and knowing the truth, found it necessary, as he says himself, to commit perjury and corroborate the Joyces, as the only condition upon which "he could save his neck." On the 4th of November, ten days before the trial, Philbin entered into treaty with Mr. George Bolton and offered to give evidence. Assuming that he had no knowledge of the murder, it was very easy for him at this date to corroborate the story of the Joyces, for he had heard them repeat it at least six times in evidence, and heard it still more frequently in the reading of their depositions.

I shall not attempt to say how often or how long Mr. George Bolton and Mr. Anthony Philbin met in conference—for I am examining the case, not upon Philbin's recent confessions, but solely upon the admissions of the Crown. It is agreed, however, that he made a deposition on the 9th November, and another—presumably an improved edition—on the 10th, Mr. Bolton being the witness to each. What can be said for the administration of law in this country when we have the plain fact before us that counsel defending wretched peasants charged with this brutal murder were forced to proceed with a farcical trial without ever having been supplied with copies of these depositions or that of Thomas Casey, the other approver? Could there be anything more essential in securing a fair trial; anything more adequate to the vindication of truth and justice, than that those men should be cross-examined upon the statements which they had made? Yet I find that counsel applied for an adjournment of the case, grounding his application upon the fact that he had not got copies of these depositions, and the application was refused. No rational man who compares Philbin's depositions with the evidence he gave in the witness chair, and the evidence of the other witnesses, can have any doubt on his mind that Philbin falsely swore himself a murderer to save his wretched life. Let me give an instance. Describing what was alleged to have taken place at Michael Casey's house, he says several times that he passed "below the house," clearly showing that he was under the impression Casey's house was to the right of the boreen when it is actually situated on the lower or left side. The three Joyces say they saw the six men go into this house, and that they (the Joyces) waited for them to the rere of the house at a spot which the civil engineer proved was seven yards from the house. But here is Philbin's testimony:—

"When we went to Michael Casey's house they went in and I went round behind the house. . . It was not many yards from the house—not more than ten."

Thus we have this man placing himself in the very identical spot that the three Joyces say they occupied in wait for him and the five others whom they allege they saw enter the house. It really seems providential that of all the places which he could select from in his perjured testimony he should put himself into that one alone which would make his evidence and that of the Joyces incompatible. Again, coming to the events which occurred at the house of the murdered family, the Joyces deposed that they stood in front of the door at a bush, which I have ascertained to be 50 feet from the door; and that after hearing the first shot they ran away.

Here is Philbin's evidence as to that point of the case:—

"I stood out in front of the door. There were two or three men between me and the men who broke in the door.

"Where were you standing when they broke in the door? About three or four yards behind them, and I then moved out 'fornent' the door.

"Did you remain below the house? When the men broke into the house I broke and advanced away.

"Had the men gone into the house before you went away? They had. *When I heard the screams and shot I went away the nearest way.* I got frightened.

"What do you call the nearest way? Any way that it was my advantage to go.

"Did you go back the way you came? I went the best way.

"Was that the way you came? I went through other fields to take the nearest way.

"When going home did you meet anybody? *No sir, nor did I hear any footsteps.*"

Here, too, it will be seen, he places himself in direct conflict with the testimony of the Joyces. They ran when they heard the first shot. So did he. Yet they never saw him. He, the innocent and unsuspecting murderer, never saw them, *nor did he hear any footsteps*, even though the nearest way, which he alleges he took, must necessarily bring him through the identical spot where they allege they were, and though, according to their evidence, they must have started off to run at that same moment.

In the deposition which this man made when closeted with Mr. George Bolton on the 9th November, and for the first time brought to light in the Under-Secretary's memorandum, the following passage occurs :—

"When we (Thomas Casey and himself) crossed the river some distance at Cappanacreha we saw three men coming down the field. After some time these men came on to the road where we were. They are Myles Joyce, Patrick Joyce, and Patrick's son Tom; but I did not know him at the time. We walked on towards Casey's. When we were near Casey's house Martin Joyce came to us."

Now this was evidently an inconvenient way to lay the plot. Meeting Martin Joyce when coming near Michael Casey's house would only bring five men past the house of Anthony Joyce, and virtuous Anthony had sworn to six. Accordingly we have it on the testimony of Sir R. G. C. Hamilton, Under Secretary, that Mr. George Bolton is at the jail again next morning, and Mr. Philbin and himself sit down to another deposition, the corresponding passage of which is made to run thus :—

"After we crossed the river at Cappanacreha we saw three men coming down towards us. They joined us after some time. They were Myles Joyce, Patrick Joyce, of Cappanacreha, and his son Tom. We walked on some distance towards Derry, and *after some distance* Martin Joyce came down through the fields, and we all went together to the house of one of the Caseys of Derry."

The alteration is slight, but the improvement is great, and few can fail to appreciate the nice distinction between the phrases "when getting near Casey's house," and "after some distance." One is definite and dangerous in cross-examination. The other is beautifully indefinite. As to cross-examination, however, "assurance was made doubly sure" by giving neither of these depositions into the hands of the defending counsel.

Yet still another slight improvement was called for. In the deposition made on the 9th, Philbin says :—

"There *were others about Casey's* house joined us, and we went down under Casey's house. I asked Martin Joyce where they were going."

He must evidently have a bad memory, for six times or more the Joyces had sworn that they went *in* to the house. But the point is made all right when Mr. Bolton visits him next day, and in the deposition dated the 10th, the passage runs thus :—

"We all went together to the house of one of the Caseys of Derry. They all went in except myself. I remained outside. They only stopped a short time in when they came out."

What a skilful retouching! There is evidently the hand of an accomplished artist here. The Joyces are corroborated in the main. But why not in the full? Why not Anthony say he had gone in himself too? Silly question. If Anthony had said that, how did he know that there was not an element of truth in the story of the three Joyces, and that some one or more out of those who may have been in that house should not come forward and declare him a liar and perjurer by showing that he was not in the house at all? No; he wisely left himself outside in his story, for no one but the accused could contradict him so far, and their mouths were sealed.

The difficulties which Casey encountered when on the first day of the trial he came to assist the Crown must have been very great. The Joyces had told a story so manifestly false that, though he was willing to give evidence, and "save his neck," it was not easy for a man who knew the truth to corroborate a story so absurdly false as to every essential circumstance. They had not described the route, for the murderers when together scarcely came within two miles of Michael Casey's house; they had set down ten as being present when only seven were actually there; they swore against six who were innocent and only four out of the guilty; they deposed to recognising them as they passed them on a dark night, when in reality the men had blackened faces; and, in addition to all, Philbin in his information had further complicated matters by his absurd ignorance of the locality and the position of houses in the few additional particulars he had to supply. To keep from mixing in the bitter and unnecessary truths with the falsehood which alone was required must have been no easy task to a man who knew all, and it will be difficult to account for his success if we reject (as, of course, we are bound to do) the explanation he gave me himself—viz., that Mr. Brady and Mr. Bolton read Philbin's deposition for him, and enlightened him.

Yet, notwithstanding all, he brought two new names, that of Pat Kelly and Michael Nee, into his depositions. Of course, this was done on the first morning of the trial, and it was not possible to visit him on a second day and have a revise of his deposition. He had to mount the witness chair. The Joyces swore there were ten men, and only ten, in the murder party. They were cross-examined, and said it was not possible that any one else could join the party on the way. Philbin swore ditto. He "was one of the ten himself, and no one could join without his seeing them." But here is part of Thomas Casey's deposition:—

"We went down the boreen after we left Michael Casey's house. About a quarter of a mile from Michael Casey's we were joined by two men, Pat Kelly and Michael Nee. We all went to John Joyce's house at Maamtrasna."

And yet, this is corroboration—this is the "clear and unmistakable testimony" we have heard so much of, and by which one innocent man was strangled on a gallows and four more innocent men lie in jail. Upon what possible theory, it may be asked, was so contradictory evidence acted upon? Surely one or both of these men who say they belonged to the murderous party must be a perjurer. The Crown, of course, it will be said, rejected Casey's testimony as unreliable, and adhered to Philbin, who corroborated the Joyces. Not at all. The Crown relied upon both, and the introduction of Kelly's and Nee's names, inconsistent as it was with the other testimony, was the delightful theme upon which Judge and prosecuting counsel descanted in endeavouring to give the murder an agrarian or political character. Here is how the Judge (Lord Justice Barry) who presided at the trials dealt with the difficulty thus raised—

"Neither Kelly nor Nee was now on trial. They were not arrested. It was curious that Philbin said he never saw them at all. The question was whether Thomas Casey was telling the exact truth about it. It might possibly be suggested that knowing Kelly and Nee were the authors of the dreadful act, the persons who issued these mysterious orders, and could have these orders obeyed, he wished to bring them into it, although they might not have been there at all. Of course, if they thought Thomas Casey was not telling the truth, the safest way to deal with his testimony would be to reject it altogether. But if they found him corroborated in the main facts it would be for the jury to say if it was impossible or improbable that Kelly and Nee were the instigators and concoctors of the whole thing; and that they were lurking on the way and joined the party."

Comment upon this is unnecessary.

CHAPTER V.

THE TRUE HISTORY OF THE MURDER.

REVELATIONS OF THOMAS CASEY, THE APPROVER.

IT is now an open secret that the officials of the Crown who had to deal with the Maamtrasna trials were sadly perplexed to ascribe a motive for the barbarous murder out of which they arose. Family quarrels and private feelings of revenge were motives that would naturally suggest themselves to sober inquiring minds, but these were not to be thought of at a time of deadly conflict between the Land League and the Irish Executive, and the Government official who would allow a murder of that special enormity to pass without availing of it to blacken the character of the Land League would be unworthy the confidence of his employers. So universally was this feeling appreciated in Irish official circles that ordinary social crime seemed during the period of the agitation to have completely disappeared.

The strange story of the Joyces did not help much in giving a political or agrarian complexion to the murder, and so official fancy had to be called into play. Maamtrasna is in the county of Galway—so is Cloughbrad, the village where Lord Ardilaun's two bailiffs had been previously murdered. Here, certainly, was sufficient foundation upon which to build a motive. The murdered family of the Joyces must have looked on from a hill somewhere in Galway county and witnessed the Lough Mask murder committed somewhere in the same county. No more intelligible motive presented itself to the official mind, and therefore this must be the only one. Many miles of distance and intervening ranges of hills were obstacles of small account in the official investigation, and this was fully accepted at the time as the theory of the Maamtrasna massacre. It is scarcely necessary to say that fancy never conceived a motive more absurd, and none are more ready to discard it now than the officials who once held it as gospel.

On the day succeeding the murder of the Joyce family the local police took a step which is of some importance now in considering the revelations recently made by Thomas Casey, the approver. Recalling to mind the unhappy quarrels about sheep between the murdered man and a neighbour of his, they arrested, on the morning after the murder this neighbour. But as a policeman in the district expressed it to me, they were forced to release him when the story of the three Joyces was accepted. This fact is no secret in the district. Everyone there knows it, and everyone, police and people, know that this is the person Thomas Casey, the approver, has referred to in his recent revelations as having planned and paid for the murder. I am fully alive to the responsibility I incur in dealing with this branch of my investigation in the same unreserved manner that I have dealt with it hitherto.

But having fully satisfied my own mind as to the justice and policy of my course, 1 shall hold nothing in reserve, and will give, in the accompanying interview, the names and facts as I got them.

My interview with the approver, Thomas Casey, partook more of the character of a cross-examination than the ordinary "newspaper man's" interview. Those who read it will find, I think, that I have asked him the questions they would have asked in order to arrive at a clear understanding of this extraordinary case.

Only very few words of explanation are necessary. In the first place, even beyond the evidence of this approver Casey, I have got proof that a sort of "Ribbon Society" existed in this district. The murdered man seems to have belonged to it, and so did the seven, or at least six of the seven, who carried out the murder. This society was under the control of Pat Joyce, one of the men who has been executed, and it would seem that he was a man of very bad character always, who was ready to use this society in the interests of any one who paid him.

This fact, as well as many points of difficulty that have presented themselves to persons who took an interest in this case, will be explained in the following

INTERVIEW WITH THOMAS CASEY.

Having procured from this approver explanations of portions of the case at different intervals, and found many of them verified by my inquiries, I had a long interview with him, in which he made the following statement :—

On the night of the murder I joined the party at the house of big John Casey, of Bun-na-cnic.

Is that the man by whom you say the murder was planned? Yes.

Was any one with you going to the house? No. I went by myself across the hill from Glensaul to Bun-na-cnic. I never touched on Cappanacroha or Derry at all. When I reached big John Casey's house at Bun-na-cnic, his son, John Casey, jun., met me outside, and gave me a white *bawneen* to put over my head going in, to make sure that no one would see me passing through the kitchen.

Were there any people in the kitchen? The light was out there, and I cannot say whether any persons were sleeping there. This young John Casey met every man outside as they came, and he gave them a bag or bawneen passing through the kitchen into the room.

Were there any persons there before you? Yes, the two John Caseys, father and son, and Pat Leyden. The men that came in after me were Pat Casey, Michael Casey, and Pat Joyce, of Shanvallycahill. They were brought in separately, and had their heads covered.

Were there any more in the party that night? No.

Did the seven of you remain in the house for any time? Yes, they took a good deal of drink. I was the only one who did not take any drink.

Was that the night you planned the murder? No, we had planned it before, and met to go and commit it. This was about three weeks or four weeks before. We met then, too, at big John Casey's house (Bun-na-cnic), but as he was not there we refused to go. We believed he remained away so that he would be out of it himself, and then we would not go as he would not take part in it.

Who gave you word afterwards that the murder was to be committed? Pat Casey, the man that was since hanged. He came to Glensaul to my place at four o'clock on the evening of the murder, and told me that they were to meet again that night.

Did anyone see him? Yes, my wife saw him, and was speaking to him.

Did he wait for you? No; he went back by himself.

Did you know what purpose you were called for? I did. I knew it was to carry out the murder we had planned.

What is the name of the man that you stated some time since was pulled out of bed and asked to go with you? John Joyce. He is a nephew of big John Casey's, sir, but still I don't think he'll deny it.

Does he also live at Bun-na-cnic? He does; he lives very near John Casey's house.

Did he know you? He did, very well; and he knows Pat Joyce would shoot him only for me, when he said he had a pain and could not go with us.

KELLY AND NEE.

You have never properly explained why two of those men got false names. Had you no false name given you? No, sir. Three men got false names—the three men that were appointed to go into the house—Pat Joyce, young John Casey, and Pat Leyden. They wanted false names, so that they might call one another inside if they wanted help from one another.

Did any others get names except those three? No. It was Pat Joyce that proposed that they should have names, and he then gave himself some strange name, that I can't remember. Leyden was Kelly, and John Casey, jun., was Nee.

Was not Pat Casey in the house? He was, but I don't think he was appointed to go in at all, though he went in.

Did you draw lots as to the men that should go in to commit the murder? No, sir. John Casey pointed out the men who were to go in.

Is this the father? Yes.

HORRIBLE REVELATIONS.

Were you not the greatest stranger in the party; did you not live farthest away, and why were you not asked to go into the house? Well, John Casey asked me, too, but I would not go.

But as you were the greatest stranger, why did they not press you, or why did you not go yourself? Sure, they were all strangers, sir.

How could they all be strangers; did not some of them live close to the house of the murder? They were all strangers, for they had blackened faces. I had no disguise only a soft hat tied down over my face, for I had a longer distance to go home than any of the others. But they were all blackened. It was young John Casey blackened them with polish (blacking) in his father's house. Some of them had *bawneens* (white jackets) on them going to the house of the murder. Pat Joyce had his hat tied down over both his cheeks to cover his beard, and his face was black also. I had a stick in my hand. Two or three of the others had revolvers.

By what road did you go from John Casey's to the house of the murder? We came down the path from Bun-na-cnic, crossed the road near the new school, and along the path to Maamtrasna.

What position did you take at the house of the murder? I stood outside at the gable of the barn, and Michael Casey stood there with me. Five men went into the house, and big John Casey held the light while the other four were killing them.

What light did he hold? He had a lamp which he carried from his own house.

Did you think they were going to murder the whole family? Well, I knew then that they were, for Pat Casey and I asked that nothing would be done to the women or children, and John Casey said that it would not be safe to spare them if they were only the size of "a top-coat button."

This man is still living at Bun-na-cnic? He is, and his son also.

He has the name of having a good deal of money? He has; he is well off, and he lends money to some of the neighbours.

The whole seven of you who were present at the murder were Caseys except two men? Yes, all except Pat Joyce, of Shanvallycahill, and Pat Leyden.

None of the Joyces of Cappanacreha knew anything about the murder? No, sir, not one of them knew anything about it.

They were not at your first meeting? No, they never knew anything of the business.

THE MOTIVE.

You have said that when you all met at John Casey's house, Bun-na-cnic, the first night you refused to go to commit the murder because he was not there? Yes, sir.

Now, did you at that time appoint the night for your second meeting? No.

Was there no understanding as to meeting again for the purpose? It was understood that they would meet again when John Casey was ready to take part in it himself.

Then how did the men know they were to gather on this night? It appears, sir, that they were working together that day (the day before the murder) at Cappanacreha with some other people, and they gave word among themselves that they would go that night.

Where were they working? I can't say it of my own knowledge, but Pat Casey told me when he came for me that they were together that day making a barn for young John Casey, of Cappanacreha.

He is one of the men in jail at present? Yes.

He was not at any of your meetings and knew nothing of the murder? No, sir. Some one proposed at one time to ask him to be one of the party, and Pat Casey said that it was better have nothing to do with him, that he had a bad cough since he had the measles when he was a young lad, and would be easily known.

Were any of the two Caseys from Bun-na-cnic at the making of the barn—either the father or son? I can't say for certain, but I am sure some one of them must be there or the word would not be given.

You have already stated that you had received money from John Casey at Bun-na-cnic before these meetings? Yes.

Now, when you all met and arranged this murder, was there no other charge made against Joyce, the murdered man, except stealing sheep? Yes, there was. Himself and Casey had quarrels about sheep, and were at law with one another. But John Casey said that John Joyce made three attempts to shoot him, and that he could not live in the country with him.

Was there not some Ribbon Society among you? Yes (hesitatingly).

Is it true that John Joyce, the murdered man, belonged to it? He did; they said he was their treasurer, but I did not know much about it, as I was only three months home from England.

Who was the head of the society? Pat Joyce, of Shanvallycahill.

How did you come into it when you were only a short time at ome? Pat Joyce knew me in England?

Had this society any connection with any other society in Ireland? No. I knew nothing of any society in Ireland, but we used meet one another in England.

When big John Casey said that this man, John Joyce, attempted his life, why did you not advise him to give information to the police, and have him arrested? We did, too, but the son said that this Joyce threatened to give information against them, and he would hand over their names to the police for being in the society.

Was there anything said about his not accounting for some money he had? Pat Joyce said so.

This Pat Joyce, I believe, was what you call "a bad boy" here? Well, indeed, he was not very good.

Was every one of you who had a part in the murder, or was present at it, related to John Casey? Yes, it was said they should all be friends.

How Anthony Joyce Framed his Story.

Can you tell me whether Anthony Joyce belonged to the society? I never heard that he did.

Must he not have heard something about your first meeting? Perhaps he did, but very little he knew.

How do you account for his hitting upon some of the right men? He put in the names of all these men because they were always quarrelling with him and his brother.

But you had no quarrel with him; how did he come to make the charge against you? Oh, I'll explain that. I asked him in Irish before the magistrates, at Cong, the first day—"Why do you swear all this against me, Anthony Joyce. I never did anything to you?" He said—"Let you hold your tongue, Tom Casey. You have no need to talk, for I saw Pat Casey going over for you in the evening. He went over across the Slieve barefooted."

I suppose he knew that Philbin and you were related? He did; he knew well that Philbin was my brother-in-law, and I suppose that is why he mentioned his name.

Was Philbin in the society? He never was, sir, and never knew no more about the murder than the child unborn.

Are you aware that Pat Leyden is a nephew of Anthony Joyce's? I think he is, but I am not sure.

Where is Pat Leyden now? He went to England some weeks ago.

Now, I have heard something about a murder having been planned for the 29th of June, the day of the Toomakeady fair; did you hear anything of it? No.

You remember Toomakeady fair before the murder? I do.

Was there any plan for that night to murder this man, John Joyce? No; but I heard that there was a plan made to beat Anthony Joyce at the fair on account of some difference with Martin Joyce, one of the innocent men now in jail. This was about six weeks before the murder.

Now there is one portion of the evidence at the trial which influenced the judge very much. Constable Bryan swore that on the way to Clonbur Pat Joyce asked him was Anthony Philbin taken yet, and if he was arrested was it to Ballinrobe he would be brought. This was before the constable himself knew that Philbin was arrested. If Philbin was innocent of the murder, how could Joyce ask that question? I can explain that, sir. Philbin was arrested in the middle of the night. He is my brother-in-law; and in the morning at daybreak, Mrs. Quin, his mother-in-law, came to my house telling me that Philbin was arrested, and asking me to go into town and do something for him, or go bail for him. She was in my house when the police came in and arrested myself. Pat Joyce and I were conveyed together to Finny, and I told him this on the way. I told him that they must not have much information when they arrested Anthony Philbin. Well, you see this Joyce was a smart talkative fellow, and he thought it would be a good thing to put them astray by asking a question about Philbin, as he knew nothing about it.

Then it is not true, as the policeman swore, that you and Pat Joyce were not allowed to speak? It is not true. He knew very well that we talked, and he could not prevent us. He separated us for a while on account of our being talking, but he let us together again at Finny, and afterwards at Clonbur.

At what part of the journey did you tell this to Pat Joyce? It was going down towards the new school at Derry.

Will Mrs. Quin remember this if I ask her about it? I am sure she will, sir, and she will tell the truth about it too. If you examine my story you will find every bit of it true. I have no interest now only to tell the truth.

You got some money from this man John Casey, of Bun-na-cnic? I got £3 from his son before the murder, and £4 since I came out of jail. My wife also got £6 from them while I was in jail. He gave it for my defence.

Did he give any money for the defence of the other men? He gave money to defend all those who had any hand in the murder, but he gave nothing to the families of the people that were innocent.

How Informers are Made.

Now I want from you, as clearly as you can, the full story of your interviews with Mr. Bolton. Did anything happen with regard to your informations before you wrote the note to Mr. Bolton on the 11th November? Yes. Several days before that—I think it was on the 6th—Philbin and I were put together into a yard. There was no warder with us. He had written to Mr. Bolton at this time, and Mr. Bolton was after being with him that day. If I remember rightly, that is what Philbin told me.

Who put you into the yard together? It was the chief warder. I do not know his name. He was a stout young man with a fair moustache. I think he is now in Mullingar, for he was removed before I left Kilmainham.

Could you remember whether he was called Mr. Coulter? No. I don't think I ever heard him called by his name at all; but I would know him well if I saw him.

Was it he took you from your cell on this day? No. I was taken out of my cell by another warder, and when I came out I saw Philbin out of his cell too. We were brought by this warder to the end of the row of cells. The chief warder was there, and then he took us down and opened the door of the yard for us himself, and locked us out there.

Do you remember the warder that took you to the chief warder? I think his name is Moore. The chief warder said, when he was putting us into the yard—"Go in there and have a talk together." I was surprised, and asked Philbin why were we allowed there together. He said it was that we might give evidence. We were more than an hour in the yard together. No one came near us all that time. Philbin was trying to get me make a statement. He was all the time saying that I knew all about the murder and I denied it.

How did he know that you were anything more guilty than himself? He must have suspected it from seeing me whispering with the other men when we got together, or were going in or out in the van.

Had you been in a van before this? Yes, and we were remanded. Philbin told me that he was speaking to Mr. Bolton, 1 think he said that day, and that it was better for me to make a statement and save myself. One of the warders told me the next day that Philbin had turned. No friends were coming near me, and I was getting afraid. On Friday or Saturday after this I wrote the note to Mr. Bolton asking him to come to see me. I was brought out to the office to see him that day.

Is this to the Governor's office? It was upstairs over the Governor's office I was brought. The warder that brought me to this office was a tall man with black whiskers. I don't know his name. He was a sort of a carpenter, I think, for I used see him doing jobs in the jail. There was no clerk in the room, and the Governor or any other person was not there except Mr. Bolton. The warder came as far as the door with me and then stood at the door while I was in. Mr. Bolton was sitting down with his shoes off, warming his feet to the fire. He said, "Well, Casey, are you going to make a statement," or something like that. I made an effort to save those that were in. I said "The men that did the murder are outside yet, and these men in here are innocent." He said he had more than that from the Joyces and from my brother-in-law, Philbin, that Philbin swore I went to the house for him and that he met me in the field. I am not sure whether it is then Mr. Bolton read Philbin's statement for me, but I am quite certain that he read it for me. He would not accept my statement, as I would not make it agree with my brother-in-law, and he called the warder and sent me away.

MAKING DEPOSITIONS.

The trial was to come off on Monday. I saw the Governor on Sunday evening, about four o'clock, and I was talking to him. I told him about my meeting with Mr. Bolton.

Had you made up your mind this time to corroborate Philbin? I was making up my mind for it, but I was putting it off to the last moment. The Governor said to me if I wished he would speak to Mr. Bolton. I did not then give a decided answer.

The next day was the day of the trial. When we were going into the van I saw Philbin going away in a cab. The other men went into the van. I was the last to go in, and I then said to the Governor that he might speak to Bolton. I had not given him an answer the night before. We were then brought to the court. The nine of us were in the room back of the dock, and my name was called. I don't remember the warder, but I think it was Moore, the same man that brought us to the chief warder. I was brought a few yards to the right, to a little room where Mr. Brady, Mr. Bolton, and the Governor of the jail were, Mr. Bolton was the first who spoke. He said, " Now, Casey, are you going to make a statement?" He pulled out his watch, and said I had only a short time. I said, " I'd like to give evidence fair." He replied that I " had only twenty minutes to consider my neck." Mr. Bolton asked, " Who are the three men that went into the house?" I did not answer fast enough. I did not know who to say. Mr. Brady then said, low, across the room to Bolton, " I know them—Pat Joyce, Pat Casey, and Myles Joyce." Then I knew what names I should say.

Did you consent to give evidence before this question was asked? I had consented, but I did not know what to say. We were then brought out to another room. Mr. Bolton took the pen in his hand, but when I had made a small part of my statement he went away, and Mr. Brady then took my deposition.

After I had a little of it made, he read part of Philbin's depositions for me.

" Question—Can you tell me which of the two depositions he read for you?" (Here I read Philbin's depositions of 9th and of 10th November, as given in the memorandum of Sir R. G. Hamilton).

" Answer—It was the one of the 10th, for Durkan's name is mentioned in that, and not in the other. When Mr. Brady read what Philbin puts down about Durkan, I said ' That is a lie.' "

Why did you say this? Was not all Philbin's evidence a lie? It was, but I did not want to implicate anyone else who was not in jail. You will find this is true ; and when Philbin was examined in court afterwards, they never asked him a word about that part of his deposition where he brings in Durkan's name, for they were afraid I would contradict it.

" You have pointed out to me that the depositions were read for you as far as that part where Myles Joyce, Pat Joyce, and Thomas Joyce are brought into it? If Mr. Brady stopped there how did you know how to put in Martin Joyce? I first did not know how to do it either, but Mr. Brady said—" Did not Martin Joyce come down out of the field to you?" And I said yes.

Why did you bring the names of Kelly and Nee into this deposition if you wanted to have it like Philbin's? I'll tell you, sir. When I was first speaking to Mr. Bolton, as I told you before, I said to him the people that committed this murder and planned it are out yet, and I put in those two names in my deposition to make that statement all right. He was more anxious for that than any other part of my statement. When I signed the deposition Bolton, I think, came for it and took it away to the court.

While he was away I was standing with a warder in the passage. When he came back, Mr. Bolton took me into a room by himself. It was an office. He asked me a lot of questions then about Kelly and Nee, and I gave him wrong descriptions of them. He asked me about England and was I in any society there. Philbin had told him privately that I was in a society there.

Out of the ten men sworn against by Anthony Joyce and his brother, only four, you say, had any knowledge of the murder? Only four, Pat Joyce, of Shanvallycahill, who was executed; Pat Casey, who was also executed; Michael Casey, who is now in penal servitude, and myself.

Now, I want you to name the men accused who were innocent? Myles Joyce, the man who was executed; his two brothers, Pat and Martin, who are in penal servitude; Tom Joyce, Pat's son, who is in penal servitude; and little John Casey, of Cappanacreha, who is also in penal servitude.

That is the man who had a cough for years? Yes.

Of the seven men who did know of the murder, and took part in it, three are still at large besides yourself? Yes. One is in England, and the other two are here in the country.

Then there are four innocent men in jail and one guilty? Yes, sir.

And of the three who were hanged one man was hanged in the wrong? Yes sir. Myles Joyce knew no more of that murder than you did, but sure you may say they were all hanged in the wrong, for the evidence against the guilty as well as the innocent was all a lie.

Here closes my interview with the approver Thomas Casey. His shrewd intelligence and the keen desire which he evinced to elucidate every point of difficulty that I drew attention to in the report of the trials, struck me very much, and by none was I more strongly impressed than by the remarkable observation with which this interview closes. I should also mention that in addition to the facts set forth in the foregoing interview, Casey revealed to me the place where at present are concealed the revolvers which were used at the murder. Of the circumstance connected with their concealment as imparted by him I received such information subsequently as to leave no doubt upon my mind. But I refrain from giving publicity to the place or the circumstances until the Government have granted such an inquiry into Casey's revelations as will satisfy the public demand for justice.

There is scarcely a single important fact given in the above statement—minute and detailed as it is—which I do not find corroborated by subsequent inquiry, excepting, of course, the account of the jail interviews, and the conflict of testimony here, it is needless to say, will have to be judged by the public largely upon the merits of the respective characters of Mr. George Bolton, Crown Prosecutor, and Mr. Thomas Casey, approver.

CHAPTER VI.

CASEY'S REVELATIONS CORROBORATED.

FEW persons, I think, who followed my criticisms on the evidence offered for the Crown at the Maamtrasna trials, will deny that if they did not prepare the way for revelations such as those made by Thomas Casey, they, at least, discredited the singular story of the three Joyces. Grave, therefore, as must be the suspicion that attaches to a statement made by a man in Casey's position, we are the more bound to give it careful consideration from the fact that the only other explanation of the mystery offered to us has been shown to be unworthy of belief. Casey's confession and the evidence offered at the trial by these so-called "independent witnesses" are wholly incompatible. To believe one or a part of one, you must wholly reject the other. It is not a question of compromise, or of errors, or mistaken identity. In short, if Casey's recent revelations are to be credited, and I have little doubt that they will, we must regard the story told by the three Joyces as a pure fabrication, false in conception and false in every detail.

I am by no means disposed to over-rate the credibility of a man in Casey's position, and in claiming attention to the evidence I have collected in corroboration of his statement I shall not ask my readers to dismiss from their minds one feature of the odium and infamy that attach to a character like his. But he cannot be worse now than when the Crown availed of his testimony at the trial, and it will be sufficient for my purpose if readers will extend to him precisely the same measure of credibility the jury was asked to extend to him when as a self-confessed murderer and informer, he sat in the witness chair to swear away the life of his fellow man. It is a mild description of the learned judge's charge to say that he instructed the jury to accept the approver's evidence if they found it corroborated in the main. I shall ask no more; and if the corroboration I produce in support of Casey when he deposes to the innocence of a dead man be stronger than the corroboration that satisfied judge and jury when consigning living men to a murderer's death, the public, I have no doubt, will find their verdict accordingly.

First, let us take a brief general view of Casey's confession and contrast it with the theory upon which the Crown proceeded at the trials.

PROBABILITY OF CASEY'S REVELATIONS.

Even upon the ground of probability alone there is much to be said in favour of Casey's story as compared with that advanced at the trial. Does it not seem more probable that only seven men would be employed in a crime of that character than that ten would be asked where three of them at least would be unnecessary ? Is it not more probable, too, as Casey alleges, that the murderous gang was confined to one family than that they should ask the assistance of men such as Myles Joyce and his two brothers, who were first cousins of the intended victim ?

The original evidence supplied no motive ; Casey's story does. The manner of assembling, the route, the disguises, the blackened faces, the lamp carried to give light for the fell work—all combine to form a story much more probable, and certainly more circumstantial, than that related by the Joyces. Crown officials impugn the motives that underlie Casey's present action. It is said he is animated by a desire to get back into favour with the people of his locality. I certainly saw nothing to warrant this assumption, and his wish to leave the country goes far to discredit the allegation. But even if it were true, how much does it establish for the Crown ? If we must agree with the Crown that Casey's character is so bad that he now gives false evidence to win the esteem of his neighbours, can we refuse to believe Casey himself when he assures us that at the trial he gave false evidence " to save his neck," which, beyond all doubt, was in imminent danger ? If it be true that he is anxious to get the esteem of his neighbours, how do the Crown officials account for the fact that Casey should still confess himself guilty of the murder ? Would it not be as easy for him to state now that he was never present at the murder as to confess himself still guilty of the foul deed, and exculpate Philbin, between whom and himself there is certainly little love ?

But all these are generalities, and at most only go to establish a presumption. I shall pass from them to the more

DIRECT EVIDENCE OF CORROBORATION.

Casey's contention, briefly stated, is that Myles Joyce (who was executed) was innocent of all participation in, or knowledge of, the murder, and that four out of the five men in penal servitude are equally innocent. Standing on the scaffold, his eyes closed to earth for ever, and as the gifted editor of *United Ireland* beautifully expressed it, " with the rustle of the Unseen falling mysteriously on his ears," Myles Joyce himself attested the truth of what Casey now confesses. Is a solemn declaration made at a moment so awful to be completely disregarded in taking Casey's story into consideration ? Patrick Joyce, when earthly hope for him was passed, and he sought to make his peace with God, declared also under the sacred sanction of religion and in presence of the civil magistrate the truth of the statement Thomas Casey now makes. Pat Casey, under circumstances precisely similar, added his dying testimony in support of it. The solemn dying depositions then of three men corroborate the revelation of Casey. But he is also corroborated by Philbin, his brother approver. Here, then, at once, we have a case precisely parallel to that upon which the Crown moved at the trial. The two approvers agree now even more minutely than they did then in their false statement, and they are corroborated in their present testimony by "three independent witnesses," independent in the highest sense of the term, for when they gave their evidence they were beyond the influence of earthly hope or earthly fear.

Already I have drawn attention to the protestations made by the imprisoned men since they went into penal servitude, and I gave specimens of the letters in which they have always declared, in solemn language, their entire innocence of the murder. This fact in itself would be some slight evidence in corroboration of Casey, but in what a strong light does it not come out in support of him, when we find that, though there are five of those men in penal servitude only four have made these repeated protestations of innocence in their letters, and these the very four men whom Thomas Casey declares to be innocent. Here, at least, is corroboration.

But there is something more. The fifth man, Michael Casey, I find has not been altogether silent. It struck me as very strange, during my inquiries in this district, that Michael Casey's friends did not show that desire to produce his letters from prison which was so notable a feature in our interviews with the families of the other prisoners. His last letter had been given to his brother-in-law, Edward Connor, who lived some distance off, and I sent for the letter, but got back the reply that it had become torn. Well knowing the care with which letters of this character are preserved by the peasantry, my suspicions were aroused, and I came back to the district another day to pursue inquiry into the contents of that letter; and I succeeded. Michael Casey had "requested his wife to go to the master (the landlord) and to get him to memorial the Lord Lieutenant to allow him (Michael Casey) make a statement. That he was *brought into this murder by friends of his own*, who are out of jail still, and if he was to have no hope for himself, he wanted at all events to make a statement *for the sake of the innocent men who are in.*"

Here, then, is another witness ready to corroborate Tom Casey's revelations. The Crown officials can scarcely be ignorant of his desire to make a statement declaring the whole truth. Is Earl Spencer anxious that the truth should be known? If so, let him have the prisoner, Michael Casey, examined, to ascertain whether he, locked up for years in prison, and knowing nothing of Thomas Casey's confession, will give precisely the same account of the murder. How readily Earl Spencer availed of the evidence of Patrick Delaney, the murderer of Lord Cavendish, and gave him some days outing from the prison, when it is a question of obtaining a conviction upon testimony so respectable?

The fact that these men now in penal servitude pleaded guilty to the murder would, no doubt, be a great difficulty in the way of establishing their innocence, if we had not evidence so strong—in fact, so overwhelming, as that which I have quoted. But it is well, also, to consider for a moment the circumstances under which they allowed their counsel enter a plea of guilty. Three men had been found guilty, the evidence against each being precisely the same as that upon which the remaining men were to be tried. The verdict of the jury may be said to have been three times pronounced upon those men, and then they were asked to plead guilty upon promise of having their lives saved. They refused their counsel so to plead; they refused their own solicitor, and they refused the Crown Solicitor. It was only at the solicitation of their clergyman that they were finally induced to plead guilty, and what is the argument which he employed? Here it is in the rev. gentlman's own words as he writes it to me :—

"The case was then laid before me, and in the interests of the prisoners I considered it the wiser course to plead guilty. I was by no means clear at the time that they were innocent. I was certainly inclined to the belief that they were, but I had no grounds for such a belief, but their own declarations to me. I argued with myself thus—If the men were guilty their plea of guilt can do them no harm, and will save their lives; and that if they were innocent I felt that the truth would leak out, as from my knowledge of the locality and the people I believed such a huge wrong could not continue. In this way I saw a probability of these men coming back to their wives and families and homes without a stain on their character. This was the argument I made use of to the men themselves in the cell of Greenstreet Courthouse; and I dare say it was the argument which induced them to withdraw their plea of 'not guilty,' and enter a plea of 'guilty.' From this you will see that in recommending the prisoners to adopt this course I was by no means actuated by a belief in their guilt. On the contrary I rather believed they were innocent."

Have we not here a very clear and a very remarkable explanation of the course which those poor wretched men felt compelled to adopt? It is all very well for persons of noble sentiment and high mental culture to exclaim that they would face a murderer's death rather than plead guilty of a murder they never committed. But these men were ignorant, poverty-stricken, wretched peasants, to whom the choice between immediate, ignominious death and confinement with the hope of release and vindication made all the difference in the world. The course they were induced to adopt was admittedly one of doubtful policy, but I have little fear that under the direction of Providence it will turn out to have been the wiser course.

In connection with the mention of the reverend gentleman from whom I have quoted above, and who had the spiritual charge of this district at the time of the murder, there is another strong point corroborating Casey's revelations which I should not omit to mention. Again I shall give it in the reverend gentleman's own words :—

"Some time after the murder a man came to me and told me that he himself was one of the murderous gang who took part in the terrible massacre. 'Myles Joyce,' he said, was as innocent of the murder as the child unborn, and so are the greater number of those now undergoing penal servitude.' I then asked him, to see if the informers had any ground for their story, whether they passed by Cappanacreha and Derry Park, and called in at Michael Casey's. 'No,' said he, 'we did not go within a mile of that place. The Joyces story is every word of it false.' The object this wretched man had in coming to tell me his awful tale was to consult me as to what he should do under the circumstances. Though of course getting this information in no professional capacity, I shall not mention names, but you are free to make whatever use you think proper of anything this letter contains.

Can there exist in the minds of any rational man in face of such evidence a shadow of a doubt as to the main fact deposed to in Casey's revelations? With such evidence *against* a prisoner how easy would it not be for the Crown to obtain a verdict and a sentence of death? Should it be regarded as of less importance when it goes to establish the innocence of suffering men and to vindicate the character of one that has been placed beyond recalling?

I feel that I well might stop here and trust to the verdict of the public, but as I am anxious to make a complete case and to deprive Crown officials of all excuse for their conspiracy to cloak over the murder of Myles Joyce. I shall give some further evidence corroborating Casey's statement in detail.

CHAPTER VII.

Further Corroboration. The Crown Brief.

Discoveries which I have made since I commenced these chapters render it quite unnecessary for me to enter into the evidence I collected in corroboration of Casey's confession with that minuteness which I originally intended. A few leading points in his statement are all that it will be necessary for me touch upon, and I shall then pass to evidence of a character no less calculated to create surprise than to carry conviction.

A very striking point in Casey's story is the incident he relates with regard to four of the murderers calling to the house of young John Joyce, of Bun-na-cnic, and taking him out to enlist him in their murderous enterprise. This Joyce is a nephew of John Casey, the alleged leader of the gang, and resides quite close to him. If Thomas Casey's revelations were all a pure fabrication, as the Crown would fain have us believe, is it likely he would gratuitously introduce an incident of this character, and, above all others, that he would fix upon a person by no means likely to offer such corroboration as would endanger the life of his uncle?

We had an interview with this John Joyce, and questioned him as to the incident mentioned by the approver. In words he refused to substantiate the approver's statement, but by his manner he convinced me and my reverend companion of its truth much more strongly than if he had expressed his agreement in words. Our queries were met first by evasive answers. "He knew nothing," "he would make no statement that would get anyone else into jail," &c.; but my reverend companion would have a direct answer. "Did these four men come to you on that night of the murder? We must have yes or no from you." At first this, too, was evaded. But a few repetitions of it brought the remarkable response (in Irish), "don't press me, Father." I need scarcely say that we regarded this as a corroboration of Casey much more convincing than if it had been directly expressed in words.

In the same way I found Casey's explanation of the manner in which Pat Joyce came to know of Philbin's arrest amply corroborated. I examined Mrs. Quinn, the woman referred to by Casey, and she stated to me that she was in Tom Casey's house at the very moment of his arrest, having arrived there some time previously to apprise him of the arrest of Anthony Philbin, his brother-in-law, which had taken place during the night, and to ask him (Casey) to go into town to see what could be done for Philbin, as the police told his wife if she had any persons to bail him it would be better for her to send them to town. She had come on this errand to Tom Casey's house, and was actually there waiting for Casey when a party of police belonging to a different station came in and arrested Casey and conveyed him to Clonbur, in company with Pat Joyce, to whom, on the way, he communicated the arrest of Philbin.

His statement with regard to the meeting of the men at work on the day before the murder was also fully verified by my inquiries, and I found that amongst those making the barn (some of whom knew nothing of the murder) were Pat Joyce, who has been executed; Pat Casey, also executed; and John Casey, jun., Bun-na-cnic, son of the alleged leader of the gang.

Another remarkable fact in the approver's confession is his allegation that old John Casey, of Bun-na-cnic, gave money freely to defend the guilty among the accused, but gave no assistance for the defence of those who knew nothing of his own criminality. It took some very minute cross-questioning of members of the different families to arrive at evidence as to this fact; but it was nevertheless, fully corroborated; and I found that upon one occasion the son of this man, in giving money to Peter, brother of Pat Casey, who was executed, said that " any money given by him or his father for the defence of Pat Casey or Tom Casey (the approver) would never be asked back."

THE BLACKENED FACES.

One circumstance alone in Casey's confession would have formed sufficient ground for inquiry on the part of any Administration really desirous to know and make known the truth. I refer to his statement that the men who committed the murder were disguised and had blackened faces. Such a fact, if clearly established, puts an end completely to the evidence at the trial, and stamps it as a fraud and a murderous perjury. There is no possible theory upon which even the most eager apologist of Crown officials can reconcile it with the evidence of the three Joyces; and, if it be true, there is no escape from the conclusion that eight men were found guilty of murder upon evidence which was a villainous and bloodthirsty fabrication. Yet of its truth I have such proof to offer as will remove it beyond the region of doubt, and shed a lurid light upon the system of Crown prosecuting in Ireland.

Anyone who glances at my interview with the approver will see that it was by a chance question in cross-examination I elicited from him this very remarkable and important item of information. It came upon me by surprise, and certainly at first raised a doubt in my mind as to the exact truth of Casey's declarations. But the manner of its corroboration was no less remarkable. Casey made this statement to me on Sunday in the sacristy attached to the Toomakeady Church, at which he and his police guard attend Mass. The next day I again visited the Maamtrasna glen to satisfy myself by inspection as to facts which he had given me in his lengthened statement. I met a police constable who was in the district at the time of the murder, and who was acquainted with the object of my visits to the glen. After some conversation about the murder the following dialogue took place between us:—

" You are aware, I presume, constable, who it is that Casey says planned and paid for the murder?" "Indeed I am, sir. It is no secret. I know it for a long time."

" Do you think this man had any connection with it ?" "I know well he was in it, sir, and so does Sergeant Johnson. He was the first man he arrested, but he was forced to let him go after the Joyces' evidence was received."

"Is it not strange that these men went to commit that murder without having any disguise?" "Indeed they were disguised, sir. They all had blackened faces, for the little boy that was alive after the murder told Sergeant Johnson and the police when they went to the house in the morning. He said the people that killed his father and mother and beat himself had blackened faces."

I need scarcely say that the testimony of the constable was to me no less a surprise than the revelation of Casey. Subsequent inquiries brought forth abundant proof. Constable Johnson will not deny that he had this information from the two boys he found living when he visited the scene the morning of the murder. Father M'Hugh, the worthy priest who was called in to attend those, testifies that one of them made this statement to him, and both were then lying in the same bed, and in a weak condition. The boy also spoke to Father M'Hugh of the murderers having *bawneens* or white jackets. John Collins, the first man who found the family at six o'clock in the morning, got the same information from them. He was examined at all the trials by the Crown. How skilfully he must have been handled in examination that this piece of evidence (technically illegal) was not blurted out! Did no one instruct him as to the injury it would do the Crown case, or had John himself acquired that legal acumen in his mountain home which enabled him to gauge its bearing? If Lord Spencer sees no grounds for inquiry, the Irish public at least would desire information upon this point. The two boys informed all the villagers who spoke to them on the morning after the murder that the assassins were disguised, and had blackened faces. Amongst those to whom they communicated the fact are Thomas O'Brien, John (Mary) Joyce, Michael Joyce, John O'Brien, Nicholas O'Brien, Martin Collins, and Peter Leyden.

But this is what Crown lawyers would call "secondary evidence." Well, fortunately, we have primary evidence of the fact, too, and such primary evidence as my Lord Spencer cannot hide by any refusal of inquiry. Patrick Joyce, the younger of the two boys, recovered from his wounds. I visited this young lad at Artane Industrial School, where, under the kind care of the Christian Brothers, he is being trained and educated, and in clear, intelligible language he fully corroborates this portion of Casey's confession. But in connection with this branch of the case I have revelations to make more startling and more damaging to Irish Crown prosecutorship than anything which we have heard from the approver, Thomas Casey.

SUPPRESSION OF EVIDENCE BY THE CROWN.

I am free to confess that when I entered upon the examination of this extraordinary case, though I was convinced of the perfect innocence of the poor man who, standing on the scaffold, declared he knew nothing of the murder, I yet was willing to admit that Crown officials were deceived by the strange fabrication of the Joyces. It may well alarm every honest man in Ireland, whatever may be his religious or political creed, when I assert that from official documents in the possession of the Crown, and by the handwriting of officials themselves, I shall be able to prove that not one, but the whole eight Maamtrasna prisoners were convicted of murder upon evidence which the very briefs in the hands of the the Crown counsel showed to be false.

A copy has come into my hands of the brief made out for the prosecuting counsel in this case and bearing the name "George Bolton, Crown Solicitor" on the back, as well as the words "Brief on behalf of the Crown." No less than four depositions in that brief state that the actual assassins had blackened faces; but though other depositions were given to counsel for the prisoners they got no copy of these, and not a suggestion or hint was allowed to be thrown out during the trial as to the disguises and the blackened faces.

John Collins, the first of the villagers who found the murdered family in the morning, was examined at the trial, as I pointed out, and came off the table without either judge or jury or defending counsel suspecting that John Collins knew a fact which made the whole evidence of "independent witnesses" and approvers a murderous concoction.

Were the Crown Counsel and Crown Solicitor equally ignorant of the fact? No, for in the briefs which they held in their hands was fully set forth John Collins' evidence at the inquest, in which the following passage occurs :—

"I then returned to the house of the deceased, John Joyce, and we then found John Joyce, Margaret Joyce, senr., Margaret Joyce jun., and Bridget Joyce, all quite dead. We then saw Pat Joyce and Michael Joyce. They were in bed. We spoke to them. We asked them what happened them. Michael Joyce then told us that he saw three men in the house. We then asked Michael Joyce if he knew the men. He said *he did not know them as they had their faces dirty*. I did not speak to Pat Joyce."

Constable Johnson was also examined at the trials in Dublin, and made depositions at the different magisterial investigations. He was allowed to make his depositions and give his evidence before the judge without a suggestion being made as to the blackened faces, and yet on the second page of the Crown brief is given his evidence at the inquest, the day after the murders in Maamtrasna, from which I quote the following passage :—

"I went into the house. I saw John Joyce lying on the floor with his head towards the fire—lying on his face—dead. I saw his wife, Bridget, in bed in the room, and the two sons, Michael and Pat, badly wounded—both able to speak. I asked Michael, through Sub-constable Lerhinan, who spoke Irish, what had happened to them last night. Michael Joyce said in reply that two or three men came into the room and shot him in bed, and that he saw one of the men take up something like a stick and strike his sister, and that he heard his grandmother screaming about the break of day. He said he got out of bed and came down to the kitchen for a drink, and said he saw his father lying on the kitchen floor; after getting the drink he returned to the bed in the kitchen where his stepmother was lying. She was then living. Before the men came into the room he heard shots. I asked Michael Joyce how many men did he see, and if he knew them. *He said no, that their faces were black*, and that there were three or four men. I then asked Pat Joyce what happened to him last night, but got no reply. I then asked him did he know them, and he said *no, that their faces were black. I asked him if they had a light, and he said yes, a piece of bog deal.* I found a bullet, which I produce, on the floor where John Joyce was lying."

One may ask in surprise whether it is possible in a Christian country that an officer of the law, who gave that evidence at the inquest on the murdered family, would be employed for weeks after in hunting up witnesses, preparing a case, collecting statements, all going to prove ten men guilty of a murder upon evidence which his own sworn testimony attests to be false? Yet this deposition stands in the Crown brief, and only a few pages later on came his deposition taken in presence of the prisoners, where all this fact is suppressed. It may not have been strictly legal to ask a question as to his conversation with the dying boy, but surely the fact remained the same, and if the omission of the question can be justified in the eye of the law, is there any justification before God for hurrying men to a murderer's grave upon testimony known to the prosecutors to be false?

But the Crown had evidence of a class which they could and were bound legally and morally to give with regard to this portion of the case. It was never mentioned during the trial that Michael Joyce, the boy who died—the young man I should say, for he was 17 years of age—made, on the day succeeding the murder, a dying deposition before Mr. Brady, R.M. The jury heard nothing of it; the judge, I presume, knew nothing of it; and the counsel for the defence certainly knew nothing of it. Yet here in the Crown brief it stands, a record now of the innocence of the prisoners and the guilt of the prosecutors.

"Dying declaration of Michael Joyce, Maamtrasna, taken by A. N. Brady, R.M., on 18th August, 1882:—

"Two or three men came in. They had black on their faces. I did see my father and my brother killed. I am very sick. I cannot raise myself up. I was a little while in bed when they came. I was asleep when they came in. I heard the dog bark. My own dog. They said something to my father. I do not know what. I have no pain at all. I was at Mass yesterday at Finney. My name is Michael. John O'Brien told me not to tell, and Michael Malley. It was last night when they told me not to tell. They swore me on a book (Irish idiom for extracting a promise) not to tell. It is John O'Brien of the Wood. I am sure of it.

"(Signed),

"A. NEWTON BRADY, R.M."

But this is not all. We have stronger evidence still. I have already stated that Pat Joyce, the younger of the two boys, survived his injuries. The Crown paraded him on the witness chair at the trial, and here is how they jinked the trick, according to the *Freeman* report:—

"The little boy, Patrick Joyce, who had been beaten on the night of his father's murder, was next brought upon the table, but through the interpreter he stated he did not know his Catechism, nor was he aware what would happen him if he told a lie. Under these circumstances the Crown did not examine him."

Of course not. But this boy had been in the hands of the Crown officials for three months, and surely even George Bolton might have told him Hell was intended for the wicked. Can it be credited, that while this pretty farce was being played before the judge and special jury, the prosecuting counsel had in the brief which they held in their hands, a dying declaration made by this boy, also on the morning after the murder, stamping as perjury the evidence upon which they were proceeding to hang eight persons? Hidden away in the last page of the Crown brief, as if stowed out of sight, comes this truly remarkable deposition:—

"Dying Declaration of Patrick Joyce, Maamtrasna, taken by A. N. Brady, R.M., at Maamtrasna, on 18th August, 1882:—

"I did not know any one who came in. I would tell if I knew. Three men came in. It was near morning. I was long in bed. I think it was about one o'clock. I did not hear any shots. I was struck on the head. I don't know who struck me. They were 'married men' (grown-up men). *They had soot on their faces. They had whiskers.* They had bog deal lights. They had a 'kippeen' each. They lit them inside in the house. I was asleep in the inside room when they came in. I got three strokes. They did not speak a word to me or to any one in the house. I think they *had no coats but 'bawneens.'* They had three old hats. I believe I am dying. I might know them again.

"(Signed),
"A. NEWTON BRADY, R.M."

This declaration was taken the day after the murder, and with a view to being used at the trial of any who might be accused of the murder. Lawyers will appreciate the legal force of the words "I believe I am dying," introduced into it. Mr. Brady, R.M., did not think this boy too ignorant to make a dying declaration, but three months later he is found to have gone so far back in Christian knowledge while under George Bolton's moral care that he could not be sworn, "as he did not know what would happen him if he told a lie." That evidently is a question of dispute among the saintly theologians of the Castle.

But was it intended that this boy should be examined? After all, may not the Crown Counsel have acted in perfect good faith in producing him on the table? Alas! again this fatal Crown brief which strayed into my hands comes up in judgment. And, oh, what a terrible story does it not reveal in a few words! This boy's dying declaration is, as I have said, stowed away in the back page of the printed Crown brief. The brief itself bears date "October, 1882," and so early as that, a fortnight at least before any trial came on, we find, printed in italics under this boy's declaration, the following direction from the Crown solicitor to the prosecuting counsel—

(*Patrick Joyce has recovered, but his evidence is worthless.*)

Now, then, we have the key to the farce that was played before the judge and jury in placing this boy on the table. "His evidence was worthless." So says the discriminating Bolton. We should all be anxious to know why, if Earl Spencer could only bring his conscience to allow him make inquiry. Perhaps Mr. George Bolton and Mr. Brady will again turn out a fresh memorandum to explain. Perhaps Mr. Justice Johnson, then Attorney-General, can smooth the difficulty, or Mr. Justice Murphy, then prosecuting counsel, or Mr. Serjeant O'Brien, Q.C., then junior prosecuting counsel?

I shall leave the public to make their comments. I freely confess I could not well trust myself to give expression to my feelings with regard to this feature of the case. In bringing these chapters to a conclusion, I think I may so far anticipate the verdict of my readers as to say that I have established my case. Let Earl Spencer refuse inquiry; let the judge who was entrapped into a wrongful sentence on a capital charge rest satisfied with what has taken place; let Mr. Bolton and Mr. Brady mutually acquit each other; the public are now in possession of the facts, and officials who would acquit themselves of the blood of the innocent will need to vindicate themselves. Inquiry was refused It rests with those who demanded it to say whether the cry for inquiry should not now give way to one for prosecution.

APPENDIX.

APPENDIX.

REPORT OF THE MAAMTRASNA TRIALS

(Abridged from the " Freeman's Journal.")

The *Freeman's Journal* of November 14th, 1882, contains the following:—

THE MAAMTRASNA TRAGEDY.

Yesterday the trials connected with the murder of the Joyce family, at Maamtrasna, in the county of Galway, on the night of Thursday, the 17th of August last, commenced in Green-street Courthouse.

Mr. Justice Barry entered court and took his seat upon the bench at a quarter past eleven o'clock.

Patrick Joyce, of Shanvallycahill, one of the prisoners, was called to the bar. He was brought up from the cells beneath the courthouse by a warder. The Crown was represented by the Attorney-General (Mr. Johnson, M.P.), Mr. Murphy, Q.C.; Mr. Peter O'Brien, Q.C., (instructed by Mr. George Bolton, Special Crown Solicitor. The prisoners were defended by Mr. George Orme Malley, Q.C., and Mr. Stritch (instructed by Mr Henry Concannon).

Mr. Malley, Q.C., said before the Jury was called he had respectfully to make an application to his lordship. He moved that this case be postponed with the object of obtaining a view of the district over which it was alleged the prosecuting witnesses pursued the prisoners in their advance towards the house in which this dreadful murder, by whomsoever committed, was committed. He moved on the affidavit of Mr. Henry Concannon, solicitor for the prisoners.

The Attorney-General opposed the motion, and after considerable argument it was refused.

Mr. Malley said it was pressed upon him that there was another matter in connection with the postponement which it might have been more reasonable and convenient for him to have opened with. He found that there had been a notice (upon which he now grounded his application) announcing that one of the prisoners would be examined on behalf of the Crown against the prisoners. That notice had been served upon them at a quarter past two o'clock on Saturday, and was dated Saturday, the 11th of November, and it stated that Anthony Philbin, one of the prisoners would be produced to prove that he went with three of the prisoners to Joyce's house, and that they broke into the house. They had served notice upon the Crown, asking for the contents of the information, and were not supplied with it. Under those circumstances he asked his lordship to postpone the trial. It was rendered necessary that investigation as to this approver should be instituted; and it was rendered most essential that the prisoner

D

should not be taken by surprise. In point of fact, it was a general rule that the prisoners should be furnished with the details of the intended evidence, and that custom had not been adopted in this particular instance. Instead of that they had only received information of a most general character.

The Attorney-General, in opposing the application, said that that application was more tenable than the last motion. It was sustained upon the ground of surprise, and secondly that there was no time to countermand witnesses who had left Dublin; and lastly, that the notice served was so general that it gave no precise information. One of the persons had confessed to the crime, and had voluntarily stated all the circumstances to the Crown Solicitor. For that person, whose name was Anthony Philbin, he had entered a *nolle prosequi*; and he would prove that he accompanied three of the prisoners, Patrick Joyce, of Shanvallycahill; Patrick Casey, of Derry; and Myles Joyce, on the night that the murder was committed; that he saw the three of them break into the house, and heard screams and shots after they entered the place. In reference to the surprise on the part of the prisoners' counsel, he relied upon an affidavit made when the trial was last postponed by the solicitor for the defence, and in that affidavit the solicitor stated he had been in communication with the prisoners on the 26th of August, when he was retained. He was then acquainted with all the circumstances, and the Crown knew nothing of that evidence, until the prisoner made that confession, and it was immediately supplied to the solicitor for the defence.

Mr. Murphy said that in every criminal case it was open to the Crown to produce any witnesses who could throw light upon a case, and even upon a second day of the trial, if important information came to their knowledge, whether it tended to a conviction or an acquittal, they were bound to bring it forward. They had given the entire evidence of this informer, who said "I was one of the party who went to the house. I saw the door broken open by three. Heard screams and shots," and that was what this man would come forward to depose to.

Mr. Malley said the prisoner was entitled to a copy of the informations. He did not ask his lordship to postpone the trial on the ground of countermanding the witnesses, as they would still prove an *alibi* in reference to this man Philbin. He still proposed to produce this evidence, and no alteration had been made, but they wished to make further inquiries as regarded the antecedents of this approver. They had been labouring under the impression that this man was a true man all through, and had been under that impression up to Saturday; and had they known it sooner a different course would have been pursued, but now the entire front had been changed.

Mr. Justice Barry said if prisoners' counsel had pointed out any distinct matter of surprise he certainly, for one, would not hesitate to give ample opportunity to recover from the surprise, but as he understood a statement had been furnished, coming from a so-called approver, and he understood that his evidence would be of the same class as that on the information—

The Attorney-General—Identical.

Mr. Justice Barry said in the absence of an affidavit pointing out distinct matters of surprise he could not grant the application.

The two special jury panels, consisting of 200 names, were then called over by Mr. O'Neill, deputy Clerk of the Peace, on fines of £20, a number of the gentlemen who had been summoned were absent.

The following nineteen gentlemen were challenged for the prisoner:—

Frederick Maunders, Simmonscourt; Frederick Thompson, Breffniterrace; L. George Watson, Blackrock; Alexander Robinson, Grafton-street; William Seale, Grafton-street; John Gibbs, Pembroke-road; John Harris, Dawson-street; James Robertson, Dawson-street; William R. Jones, Monkstown; Stannus Geoghegan, Kingstown; Henry Thwaite Arnott, Ormond-quay; Joseph Lewers, Sackville-street; William Carter, Poolbegstreet; William Perrin, Northumberland-road; Charles W. Thompson, Mulhuddert; Charles Bailey, Finglas; Henry Thomas Dockrell, Kingstown;

Sir Thomas A. Jones, Mount-street; William Battersby, Westmoreland-street.

The following gentlemen were ordered by Mr. Bolton to "stand by."
Richard O'Malley, Woodlands, Santry ; Samuel Kelly, 18 Burlington-road ; Charles W. Harrison, 178 Great Brunswick-street : George Jordan, 31 Grafton-street; Christopher Kelly, 39 Upper Sackville-street; George Beattie, Donabate ; James J. Carroll, Tudor Castle, Dalkey ; Joseph Fitzpatrick, Swords ; Peter Leetch, 2 Drumcondra-road, Peter M'Cready, 3 and 4 Belview; James Dollard, 40 and 41 North Strand-street ; James Shiel, Rathcool ; Myles Kelly, Kingstown ; Charles Bewley Pim, 6 Dame-street ; Michael Hayden, South Great George's-street ; Joseph Begg, 105 Capel-street ; Patrick Gordon, 62 Middle Abbey-street : Thomas Kelly, Rathcoole ; Michael O'Reilly, Thomas-street ; Joseph B. Pim, Westland-row ; George Dixon, Kingstown ; Hugh O'Donnell, Queen-street; Francis Carr, Mulhuldert ; Ed. Malone, Lucan ; Daniel Toole, Henry-street ; James Fitzgerald, Sir John Rogerson's-quay : Andrew Thompson, Ormond-quay ; Andrew Derham, Skerries ; James Joyce, Duke-street, ; Daniel Sherwin, Hollywood Little, Naul ; Robert Richardson, Monkstown ; John Carver, Earl-street ; Frederick Keightly, Westland-row ; William Pillar, Camden-street ; Richard Mangan, Finglas ; Richard Pigott, Vesey-place, Kingstown.

The following jury was sworn—
Maurice Leonard, Leinster-road, salesmaster ; Charles J. Evans, Upper George's-street, Kingstown, shopkeeper ; William Carty, Grafton-street, jeweller ; Wilfred Fitzgerald, Andrew-street, stockbroker ; Joseph H. Ferguson. Ely-place, lodging-house keeper ; Wm. F. Lennon, Rostrevor-terrace, saddlier ; Mark A. Toomey, Stephen's-green, wine merchant; Chas. Aungier, Dominick-street, landowner ; James Beatty, Kingstown, bank manager ; Luke John M'Donnell, Merrion-square ; Luke Toole, D'Olier-street, seed merchant ; Alexander Bayley, Morehampton-road, major.

Patrick Joyce, the prisoner who had been put forward, was then formally indicted for the wilful murder of John Joyce, on the 18th of August last.

The Attorney-General opened the case for the Crown.

[The following passages of the statement of the Attorney-General are of interest as bearing upon the correspondence and arguments that have recently taken place with reference to this case.]

This murder was one of appalling atrocity. Out of a family consisting of six members, four were massacred outright, the fifth was so mortally wounded that he died the following day ; the remaining member, a little child, was battered about the head, and left for dead. The victims were the father of the house, who was fifty years of age : his wife—the second wife—who was about forty-five years ; the old woman, the mother of John Joyce and the grandmother of the children, who was eighty years old ; the fourth victim was the second son, Michael, whose age was about seventeen ; the fifth was the only daughter, fourteen years of age ; and the sixth was a little boy, who was aged between nine and ten years. The eldest son, Martin, was not in the house on the night of the massacre, the 17th of August ; he was absent on business in Clonbur, and might be dismissed from their memories. On Thursday, the 17th August, the night was dark, but fine. The new moon was about her fourth day, and therefore there was not much light.

* * *

As he had said, there was reason why Anthony Joyce thought it necessary to keep an eye upon this party, and they would see that by a cross-examination by the prisoner at the bar, because before the magistrates he asked John Joyce had he not a spite against him, and he replied that he believed there was not an outrage in the country but that he (the prisoner) was at the head of, and that he should have been hanged years ago. John Joyce's sheep had been torn and cut, and a foal belonging to him thrown into Lough

Mask, a lake that has concealed more than one mystery, and which it had given up to police justice.

* * *

The prisoner was arrested in his own house on the 20th August. The constable who was sent for that purpose was not then aware that any other person would be arrested. But apparently a guilty conscience at once struck the prisoner at the bar. He asked the constable whether he had heard that Philbin was arrested. The constable told him he had not heard it, and thereupon the prisoner at the bar made this remarkable observation : " I suppose if he is he will be taken by the Cappaduff police to Ballinrobe." Philbin was one of his accomplices in the murder of the Joyce family.

Mr. John Henry Ryan, C.E., the first witness produced a large map, drawn by himself, of the scene of the murder after three visits. He explained to the Jury the places marked upon it—the respective positions of the prisoners' houses and that of the murdered family, their distance apart, and the character of the intervening ground. He also submitted a plan of the house in which the murder was committed.

Cross-examined at considerable length by Mr. Malley, witness said the tree at which one of the witnesses alleged he was standing while the prisoners entered the house was 57 feet distant from the house. The line of vision would enable such a person barely to see men entering the house.

In reply to Mr. Justice Barry, witness stated that, having walked the route which the witnesses described they took, he believed it was possible for them to see everything they stated they had seen.

John Collins, an Irish speaking witness, for whom an interpreter had to be sworn, deposed—to Mr. O'Brien—On the Morning of the 18th August last I remember going to the house of John Joyce, of Maamtrasna. There were two men opposite the house at the time. The door was broken off its hinges. I went in and saw John Joyce lying on the floor of the kitchen, dead. I went out and told the two men, and then went to the village. I returned with some of the villagers, and we went again into the house. John Joyce's body was still in the same place as I had first seen it, and was quite naked. Bridget Joyce, his wife, was lying in the bed, dead. The grandmother and the daughter were in another bed in a little room, dead. Michael Joyce was lying in the bed in the kitchen, alive. He was able to speak, but badly. Pat Joyce, a little boy, was also alive. I asked Michael Joyce what happened him. I and ten more of the villagers then went to the police, and two constables went to the house.

Constable John Johnson deposed to the Attorney-General—I was stationed on the 18th August at Finney, a temporary station. About a quarter-past nine some of the villagers of Maamtrasna came to the station, and from what they told me, I went to John Joyce's house. I found John Joyce, whom I knew well previously, lying on the floor, his head towards the fire and his feet towards the door. He was dead and cold. There were two bullet-marks on his body—one on the right breast and another on the right side. The wife of John Joyce was lying in the bed. I examined her body. There was a large wound on her forehead, over the right eye. Her skull was broken ; she was dead. Michael Joyce was lying beside her ; he was alive, but weak, and scarcely able to speak. He had one bullet wound under the right ear, and another in his right side. I spoke to Michael through an interpreter, and he answered. He appeared to be choking. I got him a drink, after which he spoke a little better. I went to the inner room, and saw, lying on the bed, the old woman. She was stripped and dead. Her left arm was hanging down beside the bed. The flesh was off it from the elbow down to the hand. She was lying partly on her face, her head slightly upturned. I examined her, and found a large wound over her ear, in somewhat the same place as on John Joyce's wife. There was a large pool of blood about her head. Her skull was broken in. In the bed, lying behind her, was the young girl, her granddaughter. Her head was a little raised, and was beside the old woman's feet. Her skull was also broken in, and her brains were flowing out. She was also in her night dress. I saw the little boy Patsey in the same bed. He was alive, in a very weak state, and greatly frightened. I raised him, and spoke to him. His eye was closed. There were two wounds on his head—one over the eye and another above the ear. He was naked. There were two dogs in the room, and I had great difficulty to put them out. One ran under the bed, and I could not get it away for some time. When I spoke to Patsey he answered me. When I returned to the kitchen I found a small bullet—a revolver bullet—beside the body of John Joyce. There were two bullet marks on the wall over the bed in the kitchen, one at the head of the bed, and the other at the foot. In the evening, about four o'clock, I returned to the house ; Michael had just died. I was present at the post-mortem examination, and saw this bullet (produced) extracted by the doctor. It was taken, I think, from the spine. Another fell from the jaw during the doctor's examination. This bullet (produced) was found in the body of the father, John Joyce. The bullets were given by the doctor at the inquest to the sub-inspector, who handed them to me, and I have since had them in my possession. I searched the house on Saturday and Sunday, but found nothing, and on Monday I discovered another bullet near where I had found Michael Joyce lying.

Cross-examined by Mr. Malley—There were in all five bullets found, and they are of three sizes. The police hut near the house where the murder was committed has been only erected since the murder.

Re-examined by the Attorney-General—Witness was out on the night of the murder from nine o'clock till one in the morning. There was a bright starlight at the time.

THE INDEPENDENT WITNESSES.

Anthony Joyce, aged about 45 years, was next examined, through the interpreter, by Mr. Murphy—He recollected the night of the 17th August. He was not sure at what hour he went to bed that night. When he had been in bed some time the barking of his dog awoke him. He got up and went to the door, and saw six men, whom he did not know at first. He then went round to the back of his house, and he saw the six men again there. He then recognised the six men. Their names were—Anthony Philbin, Tom Casey, Martin Joyce, Myles Joyce, Patrick Joyce, and Tom Joyce, of Cappenareena. He had known four of the men since his youth, but two of them lived some distance away from him, Tom Casey and Anthony Philbin. Witness, after a time, went to the house of his brother, having nothing on him but his shirt, trousers, and a flannel vest. He went the "short cut;" his brother and nephew came out. He then observed the six men going towards the house of Michael Casey. Witness and his brother and nephew followed them. They went into Casey's house, and, on coming out, they went the back-road. The number of men at this time was ten. The other four were Pat Joyce (the prisoner identified by the witness), Patrick Casey, John Casey, and Michael Casey. Witness saw them coming out of Casey's house, and went behind a hedge. Witness went down after them, accompanied by his brother and nephew. The ten men then went towards the lake until they came to the river of Strangalone, when they crossed the river and went towards Maamtrasna. Witness and his companions were following them, no matter where they would go. He knew John Joyce's house at Maamtrasna. He saw the ten men go up to that house, and then he heard noise at the door. At this time witness, his brother, and nephew were behind a bush. Some of the ten men went in, the others remained outside. Witness then heard noise, like people beating at the door. He heard people in the house shouting and screeching. He could not distinguish the screams of women from those of men. He did not wait after that, but he and his brother and nephew ran back as quickly as they could to their own houses. Witness stayed at his brother's from that time until the break of day. He saw the police next day (Friday), about dinner time. On Saturday he was at Finney and saw some of the men taken by the police. He saw them again before Mr. Gardner, the magistrate, at Cong, and the prisoner was there. He was examined in their presence.

Cross-examined by Mr. Malley—Witness said all his clothes were off except his shirt when he heard his dog barking. He did not put on his shoes that night. He could not say which of the ten men were first into the prisoner Casey's house, but he saw the six men go in.

Mr. Malley—Did they make any noise at Casey's house? They went in as soon as they went to the door. When the ten men came out of the house he "cut" across a short way, and followed them. He saw no other men on the road up to the schoolhouse but the ten men. He was about one hundred yards from the men, and was not sure if he was two hundred. He kept to the right side while the others would be on the left. His brother and nephew kept with him all the time.

Did the ten men reach John Joyce's house (Maamtrasna) before you? Yes, they were around at the steps of the door.

Did they all rush in at once? They all did not. Only some of them went in.

Did you hear a shot? I heard a noise, and could not say if it was the noise of a gun or a pistol. At daybreak he went alone from his brother's house to his own, but his brother and nephew stood at their door watching after him. He was at the wake of the murdered family on the Friday night.

Re-examined by Mr. Murphy—The police were about the house on that Friday night, and also in the house guarding the dead bodies.

This concluded the witness's evidence, and at five o'clock the court rose.

Policemen and bailiff's were sworn in to take charge of the jurors. The hearing of the case will be resumed at ten o'clock this morning. The prisoners were removed under strong escort.

SECOND DAY.

(From the " Freeman" of November 15.)

Yesterday the trial of Patrick Joyce, of Shanvallycahill, for the wilful murder of John Joyce, at Maamtrasna, county Galway, on the night of the 17th August, was resumed in the Green-street Courthouse before Mr. Justice Barry.

Mr. Justice Barry entered court shortly after ten o'clock.

The jury arrived a few minutes later, and the foreman mentioned that they had been very comfortable on the previous night in the Gresham Hotel. They answered to their names.

The examination of further witnesses for the prosecution was continued

John Joyce, an Irish-speaking witness, deposed, through the interpreter, to the Attorney-General—I live at Derry. On the night of the murder, when I was in bed, my brother Anthony came to my house. All my family were then in bed. Anthony awoke me, and I went out with him. I saw six persons near my house, but did not know them. I saw them go into Michael Casey's house, which is not far from mine. When they came out from Casey's house there were ten men in the party. I then knew them all. When they came out of Casey's house I was able to recognise the six who had formed the first party. The names of the ten men were Anthony Philbin, Thomas Casey, Martin Joyce, Myles Joyce, Pat Joyce, of Cappanacreha, and his son, Thomas Joyce, Pat Joyce, of Shanvallycahill, John Casey, Pat Casey, Michael Casey. It was behind a bush near Casey's house that I first knew them. My brother and son were with me. The men, after leaving Casey's house, went towards Maamtrasna. I showed the gentleman who made the map (Mr. Ryan, C.E.), the route the men took and the route by which we followed them by John Joyce's house. We stood behind a bush a little outside John Joyce's yard when the party came to the house. There was a noise at the door: some of the party went into the house, and some remained outside. I heard noise in the house, but could not say what it was like—thunder or something. There were men and women screaming. When we heard the noise and screaming in Joyce's house we three went home to my house. I was afterwards present when the prisoner was charged before the magistrates with murder. He asked me some questions which I answered. Before that time some of my horses and sheep were injured.

The Attorney-General—What was done to your horses?

Mr. Malley objected to the question.

The Attorney-General—The question asked this witness by the prisoner was—"Did you and your son and your brother Michael strike me in Michael's house for killing your horses?"

Mr. Malley—That necessarily raises the question of the guilt or innocence of the prisoner at the bar of this additional crime.

Mr. Justice Barry—Oh, no.

The Attorney-General—Now, tell what was done to your horses.

The witness replied that they were injured.

Cross-examined by Mr. Malley—I could not say how long I had been in bed when Anthony, my brother, roused me. I did not put on my coat or shoes. I went out with Anthony in my trowsers, waistcoat and hat, leaving in the house my daughter, son and wife. Anthony had roused me by knocking at the door. I opened the door at once. I have dogs, but they did not bark. When I left my house I went across my green field at the end of my house. The party was in Casey's house while we were crossing this field. They were still in Casey's house when we came into Casey's garden. When the party left the house we followed them along the old road to the schoolhouse. I could not tell which of the party came out of Casey's house first or last. I could not tell how any of them was dressed. They all wore dark clothes. We were not very far behind the party after they left Casey's house, not farther than that window (pointing to a window in the back wall of the courthouse). We separated from the party to take a short-cut from the schoolhouse to John Joyce's house, but we kept them in sight all the time. When we came up to the bush the party was entering the yard attached to John Joyce's house. Some went in and some remained outside. Could not tell how many went in. On my way back from the bush to my own house I could not be seen by men standing outside John Joyce's house. They could not see me unless they met me.

To Mr. Justice Barry—We left the bush before the men came out of Joyce's house.

By Mr. Malley—We left when the murder and noise commenced in Joyce's house. Before going, however, I saw that some of the men were standing outside the door of the house. It was not day-light when we got back to my house. There was no moon. I never had a quarrel with the prisoners, but on one occasion in the winter at a dance the prisoner's son created some disturbance and I threw him out; on another occasion the prisoner followed my son with a knife and hammer in his hand; my son had no weapon; he merely had a basket on his back and was going for turf. My son told me he had to wait in a house till the police came.

At this point a juror handed down a note to the judge.

Mr. Justice Barry—One of the jury wish to know did the ten men keep close together or were they scattered.

The Interpreter—He says they were not scattered about, that they all kept together.

Mr. Justice Barry—Did one appear to be leading the others, or did they all walk together?

The Interpreter—He says "No; they all kept together the whole time."

By Mr. Malley—There were none of them much before the others.

A Juror—Ask him what made him follow the men that night.

The Interpreter—He says "To see where they were going."

Another Juror (Mr. Toomey)—Ask him where was the exact spot at which he identified the prisoner among the ten.

The Interpreter—He says it was along with the others.

The Attorney-General—Yes, but where?

The Interpreter—Behind Michael Casey's house.

Patrick Joyce, an Irish-speaking witness, and son of the last witness, in reply to Mr. O'Brien, Q.C., deposed—I recollect the night my uncle Anthony came to the house. My father got up out of bed, and I also did. My sister Mary also got up. My father and myself left the house together, and when we came out we saw some people whom we did not know at that time. I saw them going into Casey's house. The number of persons was six, and subsequently I saw ten come out of Casey's house, and I then knew them all but one. [The witness mentioned all the names of the prisoners except Philbin.] I saw the prisoner there that night. We followed them all to John Joyce's house, where we saw some go in and others remain outside. My father, uncle, and myself were near the house, near a tree, beside a wall. I heard a noise at Joyce's door, but I could not say that all of them went in. After those who did go in I heard a noise.

Mr. O'Brien—Was it the sound of voices? I heard the noise of people inside, and when we did we went home as quick as we could.

A Juror—Why did you follow these men? We followed them to see what place they were going to, and what they were going to do.

Cross-examined by Mr. Stritch—Was it mere curiosity that brought you after them? It was to see what they were about.

To see if you could get anything against them? It was.

Are you in the habit of going out to see what people are doing at night? No. We did not go out until my uncle came. There was not much noise made when my uncle was knocking at the door. He told me to get up.

At this stage of the witness's evidence his lordship remarked he had never heard better interpretation in a court before.

Witness continued—They told me to get up when my uncle came in.

Were you and your uncle on good terms with the prisoner? We were.

Had you any quarrel with him? I had no quarrel with him, but my father had, at a dance, when my father threw him out of the house. The prisoner on one occasion followed me with a knife and hammer, and I had to go to my uncle's house, where a police sergeant took me out. That was three years ago. I had a gun about three years ago. The morning of the murder I had not a gun with me, and I did not meet a girl named Margaret Casey.

Did you in the presence of your uncle Michael tell the murdered man that if he did not give up his gun you would be square with him? I did not.

Mr. Toomey (juror)—What did your uncle say to you that night he called? He said there were six men outside, and to get up and see what they were about.

To another juror—I saw the prisoner at Joyce's house the night of the murder.

Mary Joyce, a young woman, deposed, in English, to Mr. O'Brien—I am the daughter of John Joyce, of Derry. I recollect my uncle Anthony Joyce coming to the house the night John Joyce, of Maamtrasna, was murdered. I was in bed. I don't know the hour. Anthony knocked and my father went to the door. Anthony told him there were some people on the road. My father then got up as fast as he could. My father and brother went out with my uncle Anthony. They were away a good while, and came back together before the break of day. I was then in bed, but had not slept during their absence.

The witness was not cross-examined.

Anthony Philbin, the approver, was then called. He deposed, in English, in reply to Mr. Murphy—I live at Cappaduff, County Mayo. I have been at various times in England. The last time I was there for nine or ten years. I lived chiefly in the county of Northumberland. I came back to Cappaduff four or five years ago. I have a brother-in-law named Tom Casey living at Glensal. On the night of the murder my brother-in-law met me a little distance from my own house. I had gone on the evening of that day to a wake, and after my return I remained a short time in my house. I then went out to look if there were any trespassers on my land, and soon afterwards met Tom Casey. I had known the prisoner. On the night of the murder I met Tom Casey in the second field from my house, about eighty yards from my house. I live about five or six miles from Maamtrasna. On the way to Derry we met three men as we crossed the river at Cappanacreha. The three men were Myles Joyce, Patrick Joyce, and his son, whom I did not know then, but whose name I have since learned to be Tom.

Did the five of you go on together then? We did, sir, for a short distance.

Did you meet any other man? Yes, Martin Joyce.

Where were you when you met Martin Joyce? Some short distance away from my house; I don't know the land as I was only there once before.

Could you say what hour of the night it was when you six met together? It would be eleven o'clock anyway; between eleven and twelve o'clock, I dare say.

Where did Martin Joyce come from to join you? He came out from a field to us.

Where did the six men then go, you being one of them? To Casey's house.

Which of the Caseys? There are three houses close together, belonging to the Caseys. Five of the men went to Michael Casey's house, and I remained in the yard outside.

What distance was it from Casey's house to where Martin Joyce had joined you? I do not know. It was some distance. We were six in number going up to Casey's house. The five men did not remain long in Casey's house. I joined them again when they came out, and I then took notice of four other men.

Who were the other four whom you noticed? Patrick Casey, John Casey, Michael Casey, and Patrick Joyce.

Was that Patrick Joyce the father of the present prisoner? Yes, sir.

When the men came out of Casey's, you being ten in number, where did you go? We went down under Casey's house. I crossed a ditch and into a field. I asked Martin Joyce then where they were going to.

Had the prisoner, Pat Joyce, joined the party at this time? Yes, sir.

Mr. Malley—Was he within hearing when you asked where they were going?

Mr. Murphy desired to have the answer of Martin Joyce given in evidence.

Mr. Justice Barry—It is really not worth while arguing about. The real point is where they went to.

Mr. Murphy (to witness)—Where did the ten men go to?

Witness—I did not know, then, but I asked Martin Joyce——

Don't mind what you asked him; tell us where did you all go? They went away until they came to a street and a house, which I did not know.

Did you all go together? Sometimes they would be together and sometimes they would not be together; when going over a ditch or a drain they would scatter.

When you were all going on, were you in front, or in the middle, or behind? I was behind.

Who was with you chiefly? The one who chiefly kept my company was young Tom Joyce.

Had you any arms? No, sir.

Did you see any arms with anyone? I saw some when we got to the street and the house which I did not know.

What arms did you see there? I saw a revolver with one of the prisoners.

With whom did you see the revolver? With Patrick Joyce, the prisoner there.

When they came to the street and the house you have spoken of did you see them going to the door? I did, sir.

What was done with the door? They broke it in.

Where were you exactly when they were at the door? We came out of the garden by the side of the gable, and I was hindermost. There was a little wall, and we got out in front of the door. There were two or three men between me and the men who broke in the door.

Who broke in the door? Patrick Casey, of Derry, Myles Joyce, of Cappanacreha, and Pat Joyce, the prisoner there.

Did you see those three men you have named go into the house? I did, sir.

Are you able to state whether any others went into the house? I did not see any others going in.

After they entered the house did you hear any noise from inside? I heard screeches.

Anything else? I heard a shot fired.

What did you do when you heard the screeches and the shot? I got frightened; I turned round, and went away.

Did you go away by the same way you had come? No; the nearest road I could find I broke into,

Did you hear more than one shot? When I was a few yards off from "the street," I heard another shot, and I went away as fast as I could. I was frightened for leaving them.

Where did you make for? I went home, without waiting for my brother-in-law or anyone of the party. I made off as soon as I could. I saw none of them again that night.

When going towards this house how far were you and Tom Casey, your companion, behind the others? Not much; but we could not know the first man. Sometimes one or two would advance to the front, and then these would fall back to our company, and others would be in front. Nobody else joined us that I took notice of.

When were you arrested? Between the following Saturday night and Sunday morning.

Did you see Patrick Joyce, the prisoner, after the breaking in of the door and before your arrest? No; I did not wait to see anyone.

Did you see your brother-in-law, Tom Casey, next day? No, sir, I did not.

Or any of the party at all? No; I went to the wake of Peter Quinn on Friday night, and to his funeral on Saturday, and not one of the party was there.

Mr. Justice Barry—Did you know Anthony Joyce before?

Witness—I knew him by sight. I often saw him going to Mass, but did not know his name.

Did you know his brother John, and John's son, Pat? I knew John, but not Pat.

Examination, in chief, continued by Mr. Murphy—From the night of the murder up to the present have you spoken to Anthony Joyce, or to his brother John, or John's son, Pat? I spoke a word to Anthony the night I was arrested.

Was that when you heard them giving their evidence before the magistrate? Yes.

Did you put them some questions yourself then, after you heard them swearing? I did, sir.

Was that the only time you spoke to them? Yes.

On the night of the murder, after you left Casey's house, did you notice any persons at all following you? No, sir, I did not.

Cross-examined by Mr. Malley—You were brought before the magistrate? I was, sir, at Cong.

And when you were brought before the magistrate you heard Anthony Joyce, John Joyce, and Patrick Joyce tell this story? Yes.

The whole of this story of going from Derry to Maamtrasna? I did not hear them tell the whole of the story. They did not tell all that I knew.

Did they tell that they saw you going along to the murdered family's house? They did, but they did not tell the truth when they said they saw me going with the six men into the house. I do not know Anthony Joyce's house.

Did they tell the truth when they said you went into Casey's house with the five men? I did not go in.

They could not, then, have told the truth if they said you came out of the house with the ten men? I was below the house, and it was there I joined them.

How far was that? Not many yards—not much more than ten.

Did you keep that distance from them all the way to Maamtrasna? (No answer.)

Do you understand what I am saying? I do, sir.

And why don't you answer? (Question repeated.) I was up with them sometimes and behind them four or five yards. We passed over a few ditches.

Where did you cross the river? I am not acquainted with the land there. When we went to Casey's house they went in, and I went around behind the house.

Do you know the house next to the house of the murdered man? I don't know, sir. I took no notice of it.

Where were you exactly standing when the men broke in the door? About three or four yards behind them, and I then moved out "fornent" the door.

Did you remain below the house? When the men broke into the house I broke and advanced away.

Had the men gone into the house before you went away? They had. As soon as I came into the street before the house they broke in the door, and when I heard the screams and shot I went away the nearest way. I got frightened.

What do you call the nearest? Any way that it was my advantage to go.

Did you go back the way you came or not? I went the best way.

Was that the way you came? I went through other fields to take the nearest way.

When going back home did you meet anybody? No, sir, nor did I hear any footsteps.

Now you know what the three men Joyce proved against yourself, that is if their story be true? I heard them swearing.

When you were present before the magistrates did you cross-examine them? I asked them a few questions.

Was not that to show that you were not at Maamtrasna at all? I only asked them how long they knew me.

Was not that to show that you were not there at all? It was not to show that I was there. The men were not swearing anything against me.

Was it not to defend yourself that you put those questions? Everybody was asking questions.

(Question repeated).

Mr Murphy—Answer the question.

Witness—Every man was asking questions, and we were told to do so.

Mr. Malley—On your oath, were you not afraid you would be punished for this crime? To be sure I was afraid.

And was it not because you were afraid you swore against that man in the dock, and to clear yourself? It was because I had nothing to do with it myself. I did not do any harm.

When you met your brother-in-law, Tom Casey, how far were you from Derry? About three miles.

What brought you those three miles? Tom Casey told me he wanted me, and said he wanted to see the boys.

Was it mere curiosity that brought you to see him—to accompany him? I did not know what business he wanted of me.

Did you know when he said that the boys wanted you what he meant? I did not know what business he had.

Had you any talk with him? I said it was a very strange thing going so far such a dark night.

Mr. Murphy—What did he say to you? He said he wanted to see "the boys."

Cross-examination continued—Were you trembling when the Joyce's were telling the story? Of course; such a charge against anybody would frighten them.

Did you not tell me at first you were not afraid, and say "Why would I be afraid?" Why would I be afraid when I did nothing wrong?

You saw no way of getting out of it except by turning against the others? Would I be punished for another man's doings?

Did you not go that night upon your own free will? I would not have gone if I knew they were going to murder the man. I went with the men for company.

How far were you from your own house when you met Casey? About eighty yards.

Have you a family? I have a wife and four children.

The witness was further cross-examined as to whether on the night of the murder he was at a wake upon a man named Quinn. He said he was, and he denied speaking to his mother-in-law, who was at the wake. He did not tell her that his wife could not attend the wake as her infant was sick. He did not go home from the wake with a man named Cusack or with Thomas Quinn. He left the wake about nightfall; that was about ten o'clock.

Why did you leave the wake so early? I thought it was time for a respectable man to go home, unless he intended to stay till morning.

Was it because it was time to go home that you left? To be sure. He did not think he would have met Thomas Casey. He had been home, and had come out again to see if there were any trespassers, and it was then he met Casey.

Re-examined by Mr. Murphy—When Tom Casey said you were to meet the boys did you know what he meant? I did not. I thought it was with Michael Casey he had some business.

In examining one of the Joyces before the magistrate did he not give you this answer, "I never saw you do anything except that you were with them that night, and to the best of my belief if you were left where you were you would have done nothing."

The witness said he remembered receiving the answer, and added that Patrick Joyce swore he did not see him there. When going up to Casey's house they were four in number, and when leaving it they were ten in number.

Mr. Toomey (Juror)—How many men went into the house? Only three —Myles Joyce, Pat Casey, and Patrick Joyce, the prisoner. The prisoner had a revolver in his hand, and another of them had a short stick.

Judge Barry—How did they force the door? I saw them weighing against it.

Thomas Casey, brother-in-law of the last witness, and another approver, was next examined by the Attorney-General. He was frequently told to speak loudly, his voice being sometimes inaudible. He said he was one of the persons charged with being concerned in the murders. He went to the last witness upon the night of the murder. They met Myles Joyce, Pat Joyce, and Tom Joyce, whom he knew before that night. He had been previously at work in North Shields. Two other men named Neill and Kelly joined the party. They crossed the ribble and went to Joyce's house. He did not know Joyce's house before. Some of the party pushed in the door—he believed five of them. They were Myles Joyce, Patrick Joyce, and Patrick Casey, and the two other men, Kelly and Neill, who were not in custody. Could not say if the door was broken in. He heard reports of shots and then screams. That was after the men had broken in, and before they entered the house was dark, and then there was light. The screams were loud, and then there was shouting. Some of the men came out, but he could not say who they were. They were about a quarter of an hour outside the house.

Did you go away alone? I ran away as fast as I could.

Did you hear more than one shot? I heard many shots, but I cannot tell how many. Saw the last witness run away.

How long do you know the prisoner? I know him a good many years, and frequently saw him. Did not know the murdered family, nor did he know who was asleep in the house that night.

Cross-examined by Mr. Stritch—The last time I was in this court I was in the dock charged with the murder of these people.

Was it for the purpose of saving your life you gave this information? I should not like to lose my life.

Have you given this information to save your life? I have.

Have you had any conversation with Anthony Philbin? How could I have conversation with him in prison?

Did you speak with him in the dock when both of you were last there? We were talking in the dock. We have had no conversation since he gave his information. I brought Quinn to Derry on the night of the murder, but I did so by the orders I got.

Mr. Stritch—Never mind the orders now.

Mr. Murphy—He did mind them, though.

Cross-examination continued—I was only a few minutes in Michael Casey's house. The others remained longer, and I waited outside until they came out. I was longer outside than I had been inside Casey's house. I saw Philbin going into the yard of John Joyce's house. I could not say whether I went into the yard before him. I stood at the gable and Philbin stood beside me. I heard the screams from the house.

And you did not go into the house to save the people? No.

You waited outside until the butchery was over. I did.

Did you hear the shots loudly? I did.

And then you went away, when all was done? I did.

And gave information when you were about being tried, for the purpose of saving your life? Yes.

Re-examined by the Attorney-General—Be very careful not to answer this question except by "yes" or "no." Were you talking to Nee after he joined the party as you were going to John Joyce's house? I was.

A Juror—Who gave you the orders to go there that night?

Witness—Patrick Casey.

Mr. Justice Barry—Was Patrick Casey one of those who broke in the door? Yes, sir.

A Juror—When did you begin to know what you were going about on this night? I knew they were going, but I did not know it was for murder.

Did you know there was to be some sort of a row? I knew there was something to be, but I did not know what it was.

Another Juror—When were you told that? As I was going towards Maamtrasna.
Who told you? Nee told me.
Did you see a stick or a shovel with any of them? Some of them had walking sticks, but I did not see any firearms.
Another Juror—Are the people in your neighbourhood in the habit of carrying sticks? Yes, walking sticks.
You did not see a thick stick with any of them? No.
Sub-constable Thomas Finn, examined by Mr. O'Brien—I was present when the prisoner was arrested on the morning of the 20th August by Constable Bryan. I searched his house and found a trousers. It was damp, and had the appearance of having been washed. I asked the prisoner regarding his trousers, and he said it was his [white corduroy trousers produced]. Dr. Davys had the trousers for a time.

Cross-examined by Mr. Malley—I was stationed at Clonbur, and went to a temporary station at Finny for a few days before the arrest. The prisoner was arrested in his house. The trousers was hanging on a line in the kitchen, not being in the least concealed; and he acknowledged without hesitation that it was his. I was sent from Clonbur with Constable Bryan to investigate the house. I do not know what family the prisoner has. I saw no one in his house but his wife—a young woman.

Constable Daniel Bryan, examined by Mr. Murphy—On the 20th August I, with some sub-constables under my charge, arrested the prisoner. It was Sunday. I made the arrest about five o'clock in the morning. I took him to Cong. On the way he asked me did I hear whether Anthony Philbin had been arrested. I said I did not. He then remarked, " If he is I suppose he will be taken by the Cappaduff men round to Ballinrobe." This conversation occurred about eleven o'clock in the forenoon. At that time I did not know that there was any charge against Anthony Philbin.

Cross-examined by Mr. Stritch—There were four sub-constables with me. They had charge of the prisoner Patrick Joyce, and also of another prisoner named Thomas Casey, whom we arrested on the way to Finny. They were together at Finny while we changed horses, and also at Clonbur. I did not enter the conversation with Pat Joyce either at Finny or Clonbur. I did not consider it necessary to make the entry until I went to Cong. I am not bound to enter the statements of a prisoner immediately ; a delay is no harm if a considerable time does not elapse. I was too hurried at Finny and Clonbur looking after the horses and the prisoners to make the entries there

Re-examined—Cong was the first real resting place we had. Tom Casey is the Casey who lives at Glensal—brother-in-law of Philbin. I arrested him in his own house. It was when both prisoners were in custody that the conversation took place.

Head-constable John Wynne deposed to Mr. O'Brien—I went on that Saturday to search the house of the murdered man. Constable Geary found a purse containing £3 7s. I saw him take it from a trousers. I assisted at the removal of the bodies for the postmortem examination. When Michael's body was removed from the corner into the centre of the room this bullet (produced) dropped from him. It is a revolver bullet. I found it where he had been lying. There was a wound in Michael's side, and his entrails were protruding. Another bullet, quite flattened, was handed to me by Martin Joyce, son of the murdered man. There were bullet marks on the wall. The sister of the murdered man handed me two other bullets which had been picked up when the bed in the kitchen was pulled out and shaken.
The witness was not cross-examined.

Mr. John Charles Gardner, R.M., deposed to the Attorney-General— John Joyce and others were examined at an investigation which was held before me in presence of the prisoner, who cross-examined them. I asked each prisoner, including Pat Joyce, if he desired to ask any questions.

cautioning him that they would be taken down in writing, and might be used in evidence against him. Pat Joyce asked some questions. His questions and the answers given are contained upon this deposition [exhibited] of John Joyce.

The Attorney-General proposed to read the prisoner's questions and the answers of John Joyce thereto.

Mr. Malley objected to their reception on the ground that insufficient caution had been given to the prisoners.

Mr. Justice Barry allowed the evidence.

The Attorney-General—The question of the prisoner was, "Had you any spite towards me?" The answer of John Joyce was, "I believe there was nothing going on in the country that you were not at the head of. Hanged you ought to be when others were sent to gaol." The next question was, "Did you strike me in Michael Joyce's house for killing your horses?" The answer was, "I struck little at you. I cannot say when it was, in consequence of every badness you were in, that I struck you."

Sub-Inspector John W. Phillips deposed to Mr. Murphy—I recollect on August 21 firing some revolver shots in John Joyce's house. I left Mr. Gardner outside the house while I did so.

Mr. Gardner—I stood at the exact spot that the witnesses, Anthony and John Joyce, pointed out to me that they occupied on the night of the murder when they heard the screams. The sound of the shot was like a dull thud, something like the knocking of one's knuckles against the door. I then went into the house and fired shots of larger bore, Mr. Phillips standing outside where I had been.

Mr. Phillips—The sound I heard was like a soft blow upon timber. On the 23rd August I searched the prisoner's house and found this revolver case in the thatch; it was at the foot of the thatch with some rags, and could not have been observed except by a tall person or a person standing on a stool and making a careful search.

Cross-examined—I am stationed at Limerick, and was brought to Cong to assist in the investigation of this case. I was born in the county Galway, but left it when very young. The revolver cover, when I found it, was covered with dust, and appeared to have been in the thatch for some time. I found no firearms, although I searched the ditches and several houses. I did not search the houses of Anthony and John Joyce.

Mr. Gardner cross-examined—The day we fired the shots was not calm. It was blowing pretty fresh, and from where I was standing towards the house. I would never have known that the sounds were the reports of firearms, until I was told. [Mr. Malley here put into the witness's hand a loaded revolver, and was proceeding to cross-examine him in reference to it, but the Attorney-General objected to the revolver being exhibited while loaded. The witness handed the revolver back to Mr. Malley.]

Mr. Justice Barry—Do you always carry that in your pocket, Mr. Malley? (Laughter.)

Mr. Malley—I will return it, my lord, to the gentleman who had it.

(The learned counsel then placed the revolver in a green bag, and handed it to the prisoner's solicitor, who placed it on a seat before the dock).

Dr. Hagarty deposed to the wounds that were inflicted on the murdered persons.

The little boy, Patrick Joyce, who had been beaten on the night of his father's murder, was brought upon the table, but through the interpreter he stated he did not know his catechism, nor was he aware what would happen to him if he told a lie. Under these circumstances the Crown did not examine him.

The Attorney-General then announced that the prosecution by the Crown had closed.

An adjournment was then (at two o'clock) allowed for luncheon, and on esuming at a quarter before three o'clock,

Mr. Malley asked for a record of the charge first placed upon the books against the accused.

Mr. O'Neill, deputy Clerk of the Peace, said he had no record beyond the indictment upon which the prisoner was taking his trial.

Mr. Malley said he did not require that; what he wanted was the charge originally laid against them.

The Attorney-General said the indictment laid against this prisoner was the original indictment, and the other accused were included in it.

Mr. Malley then addressed the jury on behalf of the prisoner.

Michael Casey, who spoke nothing but Irish, was next examined through the interpreter. In reply to Mr. Stritch, he deposed—He was brother to the woman that was murdered. He knew Anthony Joyce. He recollected the night of the wake. Joyce spoke to him about the murder of his sister.

Did he call you aside? It was out on the hill, and he told him that he saw those men going in that direction, and that it would only be right to put them out of the country, as it was them who committed the murder.

Mr. Stritch asked leave to cross-examine the witness.

His Lordship said as yet he thought the witness was giving his evidence fairly.

In reply to Mr. Stritch, the witness said he told the solicitor all he knew about the matter.

Did he ask you to swear against them.

The Attorney-General objected, and the question was disallowed.

Patrick Keenahan, Derrypark, deposed—He resided about a mile from Anthony Joyce. He knew John Joyce and Pat Joyce. Recollected the morning of the murder. He was out on the field going up the mountain, where he met a little boy named O'Brien, who said he was coming from Maamtrasna. He afterwards met Pat Joyce (witness), who had a gun in his hand. They talked together, but Pat Joyce did not say anything about the murder. Pat Joyce was coming from the direction of Maamtrasna. It was before breakfast that witness met Joyce.

Witness was not cross-examined, and this closed the case for the defence.

Mr. Stritch addressed the jury for the defence.

Mr. Murphy, Q.C., replied on the part of the Crown.

The court then rose.

THIRD DAY.

(Abridged from "Freeman" of 16th November).

THE VERDICT—SENTENCE OF DEATH.

Yesterday, at eleven o'clock, the trial of Patrick Joyce, of Shanvallycahill, for complicity in the murder of John Joyce, of Maamtrasna, was resumed for the third day in the Green-street Courthouse, before Mr. Justice Barry.

His Lordship's address occupied three-quarters of an hour, and there seemed to be some surprise in court when he came to the words "in conclusion," as it was anticipated he would have spoken for at least an hour. The jury returned their verdict within eight minutes, and the prisoner was condemned to be hung on the 15th December.

Constable Bryan was re-called at the instance of the learned judge, in reply to whom the witness stated that it was he who arrested the prisoner; he also arrested Thomas Casey a short time afterwards, and about four miles further on. Before the prisoner used the expression that if Anthony Philbin were arrested he would likely be taken by the Cappaduff police to Ballinrobe, Casey had no opportunity of conversing with the prisoner.

Mr. Justice Barry then proceeded to address the jury. He said—Gentlemen of the jury, when I look up into that box, and recognise the faces so familiar to me, of men not to be surpassed in this city for independence of character, for education and intelligence, I shall not occupy time in making any prefatory observations with the view of enlisting your attention or of impressing upon you the solemnity of the duty which the laws of your country have on this occasion imposed upon you. Neither, gentlemen, shall I expatiate upon the enormity of the crime—into the circumstances connected with which you have been empannelled to inquire—a crime which, in its unparalleled enormity, I may say without exaggeration startled the civilised world. * * * * The next witness is one of great importance—Anthony Joyce. He says that on the night of the murder he was in bed; that he was awakened by the barking of his dog; that he went to the door in consequence of the noise; and that he saw six men. He did not recognise them at first, he said, but he saw them going towards the old road. He then retired to the back of the house, and then he says he knew them. For some reason or other, instead of tracing them by himself he went to his brother's house and called up his brother and his nephew. Several of you were very anxious to ascertain what it was that was passing through the minds of those Joyces in pursuing those six people. They did pursue them, according to their evidence. It is for you to say whether they did or not. There are great difficulties presented to jurors in the state of our laws as to what is passing through men's minds at certain times; you can only judge of that by acts. It is for you to say, as has been suggested, whether Anthony Joyce substituted the names of persons against whom he had spite for the persons he saw. It has been suggested with undoubted force that if these three men were pursuing six men, or, as it afterwards proved, ten men, that the ten could turn round and see the three. That is very possible. It is difficult to resist such a conclusion. But it may suggest itself to one's mind, on the other hand, that in the night, with three men behind and ten men in front, engaged on whatever object they had in view, the ten men may not have thought of turning round to see if they were being traced in that lonely district. The six men are seen going into the house of Michael Casey. According to the evidence of one of the informers, Anthony Philbin remained outside; but you may think that that fact, so far from raising any doubt, is confirmatory of the evidence of Anthony Joyce and his brother and nephew, who, in the night, if they saw five men going into a house, would say generally, "they went in." * * * * One of the four additional persons who came out of Casey's house is sworn by Anthony Joyce to be the prisoner at the bar. There was a suggestion made during the very able argument and speech of Mr. Malley that these witnesses may have committed this murder themselves, and, to screen themselves, had accused others. That suggestion was in a manner most becomingly withdrawn by Mr. Malley when it was subsequently commented upon. The theories, therefore, presented to you on the evidence of those Joyces are—first, that they have invented the entire story, and that they did not see the people going at all to Joyce's house; or that, having seen people going, they, with deliberate falsehood, or with reckless assertion, insisted that it was these ten men they named whom they saw. But as we were told in the magnificent oration we heard from Mr Murphy yesterday, it is a terrible accusation to bring against the three Joyces—Anthony, John and his nephew—that they concocted this story for the purpose of, at one fell swoop, destroying these ten men. The ten men did not live in their immediate district; they came from here, and there, and elsewhere. Anthony Philbin comes from a district which, according to the evidence, is scarcely known to them at all. But that is matter for argument entirely for you, and I may here disclaim any intention of suggesting any conclusion of fact to you. It is not my duty, it is not my privilege, and I will not assume the duty or usurp the privilege. You may ask—Why fasten upon these ten men out of the whole community? Why fasten upon ten at all? No doubt it is a terrible accusation

E

to bring against those three witnesses. In fact, I think we must concur in the observation made by Mr. Murphy, that great as is the guilt of the parties who slaughtered the Joyces in their wretched dwelling, their guilt would be small in comparison with the guilt of the three Joyces in coming into this court and, without any motive suggested, swearing away the lives of ten innocent men. The other theory is that, having seen the party going along the road, they falsely or recklessly asserted that the prisoner and the nine others were the persons. That is really very little less criminal, if less criminal at all, than the other hypothesis—that they invented the story. Again, it is impossible to deal with this case without considering that there is a peculiar element in it which distinguishes it from other cases— the enormity of the crime that has been committed—because in other cases you may deal with probabilities and improbabilities, but here there is one dreadful fact— that an entire family was slaughtered. * * * * It is said, and we heard a great deal of argument on this subject, that in the story that they ran back to their own house there is some degree of improbability, because they did not run to the police barrack at Finny. Well, really, gentlemen, this is one of those murders upon which men of experience and intelligence must exercise their own discretion. It is not for me to suggest any conclusion upon that subject; but I know it does not appear to me to be at all unnatural that they should run back to their homes, where they would have the shelter of their own houses over their heads instead of running the risk of coming in contact with those ten men again. I think that was a very natural circumstance, if it did occur at all. The truth or falsehood of the evidence given is entirely for you. He describes the noise he heard as some kind of thundering or screeching. The Crown gave some evidence which perhaps I dealt with as of less importance than it really was—namely, the possibility of revolver shots being fired in Joyce's house without being heard by persons standing where the three witnesses say they were standing. The evidence becomes somewhat material in view of the fact that four bullet wounds were found upon the bodies inside. I think there is a good deal of force in Mr. Murphy's statement that the fact of these men saying they did not hear the shots is calculated to raise the credibility of their testimony in the estimation of the jury; because if they were concocting a story—this is the argument of the Crown, not mine—nothing would have prevented them saying "we heard shots" when shots were fired. Their statement that they heard no shots has, as Mr. Murphy states, a great deal of force, and indicates a desire not to exaggerate or tell what is not true. Then comes evidence of considerable importance. I don't know whether it has so occurred to you, but I deem it my duty to call your attention to the evidence of Mary Joyce. It will be for you to say whether the evidence of Mary Joyce is not of great importance. You saw that girl on the table. You heard her give her testimony. If she was in the conspiracy you would probably say she would have been made to say a deal more than she did say. All she says is that a knock came to the door, her father got up, called her brother, her uncle came in, and that they all went out together, and were a long time away. Where were they? He says they were looking on at what they had described. What brought Anthony Joyce there that night, if that dog had not awoke him, and if he had not seen the six men, and why did he then call his brother and nephew and leave the place? Now that was the testimony as far as the Crown relies on, of the Joyces. Then came the evidence of a man, no doubt tainted, as an approver, Anthony Philbin. Philbin, truly or falsely, makes himself out less culpable than the others whom he says were engaged in the transaction, because his account is, that he was asked by his brother-in-law, Tom Casey, some where or other, to meet "the boys," and of course it would be idle for us to say we do not know what that meant. He says he did not know what was up, but we may reasonably assume that it was for no good purpose. He described how six of them went to Casey's house; how four more joined them there, and how they finally

came to the house of the murdered family. He states that as soon as he heard the door broken in, and a shot, he ran away. His suggestion is that he meant mischief, but not murder. Gentlemen, you cannot act upon the testimony of an informer or informers unless it be corroborated in some material matters affecting the prisoner, by independent testimony. If you believe the testimony of Anthony Joyce, his brother and nephew, it is more than corroboration. Philbin says he heard screams, got frightened, and went away, and when going away he heard another shot. The next witness was also an approver, Thomas Casey, and is brother-in-law to Philbin. He describes the transaction substantially in the same way. But says that he remained there until the murder was over, and until some of them had come out of the house. He said that the screams were loud; that he heard many shots, and that he ran away when the men were coming out. This was the man who gave that remarkable piece of testimony. He was asked why he brought Philbin there, and he says, "By the orders I got;" and in answer to a juror he says, "I got the orders from Patrick Casey (the prisoner), and he was one of those who broke in the door." Singular to state, according to this testimony two men secretly joined the party on the way. It is for your consideration to say whether that evidence bears upon the evidence of the Joyces or not. The next witness is Constable Finn. I confess that in considering the circumstance of the pair of trousers being found with a few specks of blood on it in the prisoner's house (that is, if I were a juryman) I would place very little reliance on it. However, it will be for you, gentlemen, to say what weight you will attach to that evidence. Then came Constable Bryan, whom I called up again to-day to ask a question that has been much pressing on my mind. The prisoner was arrested, and so was Thomas Casey on the same day. They were arrested at a distance from each other, and the constable says that when he had the prisoner in his custody, without there being any communication between the prisoner and Casey, that the prisoner put this extraordinary question to the constable, " Is Anthony Philbin being arrested?" The constable had never heard the name of Philbin, and he did not understand what the prisoner meant. What suggested to the mind of the prisoner that Anthony Philbin could possibly be arrested? The Crown ask you to come to the conclusion that he knew Anthony Philbin was one of the party that night. Now, supposing there was an opportunity for Tom Casey, Philbin's brother-in-law, to have communication with the prisoner, that is, supposing Casey was at the murder, and also Philbin, and the Joyce's swear they were there, why would he communicate to the prisoner at the bar any thing about Philbin or himself? * * *
But, I repeat, whatever horror you may entertain of that crime, whatever desire you may have that the guilty perpetrators of it should be brought to justice, recollect that the law requires no victim. The question for you is, has the guilt of the prisoner been established upon testimony which satisfies your consciences and judgment of his guilt? If you are of that opinion, you may be regardless of all consequences, and a true verdict give according to the evidence. If you have a doubt, you will be entitled to give the benefit of it to the prisoner. But, gentlemen, the doubt must be the doubt of firm, rational, reasonable men—no crochet, no chimera, no cowardice. I cannot believe you would be capable of such a state of mind as I have suggested. I have no doubt you will do your duty as becomes highly eminent citizens of this great city—that you will discharge your duty between the prisoner and the country, faithfully, calmly, impartially, regardless of consequences. And may God direct you to a right conclusion.

The jury then, at two minutes past twelve o'clock, retired to consider their verdict. They had been absent only eight minutes, and returned to court at ten minutes past twelve. The prisoner was brought back to the dock, and the learned judge was sent for. After about twenty minutes his lordship returned to the bench. The foreman, amidst excitement in court, handed down the issue paper. The prisoner stood up against the bar of the dock.

The Clerk of the Crown—Gentlemen, have you agreed to your verdict?
The Foreman—We have.
The Clerk of the Crown—You say, gentlemen, that the prisoner, Patrick Joyce, is guilty?
The Foreman—We do.

The prisoner received the announcement with manifest callousness. He merely brushed his right hand along the bar of the dock and looked upwards to the jury in a listless manner.

The Clerk of the Crown, in formal language, told him of the verdict of his country, and inquired: What have you now to say why judgment of death and execution should not be awarded against you, according to law?

The prisoner replied "Not guilty," raised his left hand, and for a moment pressed his cheek against it; but almost immediately relapsed into complete self-possession.

The prisoner was then sentenced to be executed in Galway jail on the 15th December.

The Crown then formally entered *nolle prosequi* against the two approvers, Philbin and Thomas Casey.

TRIAL OF PATRICK CASEY.

After an interval,

Patrick Casey, a middle-aged man, who lived about a quarter of a mile from the last prisoner, was put forward and indicted for the wilful murder, on the 18th August, 1882, of Bridget Joyce, wife of John Joyce, whose murder was the subject of the previous investigation.

The accused pleaded "not guilty," and was defended by the same counsel as in the previous case.

The following jury was sworn:—
William Wardropp, Simmonscourt; Henry T. Farrell, Merrion-square; Charles Sexton, Dawson-street; George Phenix, Temple-road, Rathmines; William Harrison, Monkstown; Samuel S. Waterhouse, Dame-street; Chas. Bewley Pim, Dame-street (affirmed); James F. Roberts, Leeson-park (affirmed); Henry Watson, Bachelor's-walk; Nicholas Hammond, Monkstown; Philip S. Barrington, Bray (affirmed); Graves C. Armstrong, Monkstown.

The Attorney-General re-stated to the jury the case for the Crown.

The witnesses were then examined in the same order as in the preceding case. Mr. Ryan, C.E., re-produced and re-explained the map of the district; John Collins, who first discovered the family murdered, repeated his evidence; Constable Johnson produced the bullets found by him in the house, and described the appearance of the victims in greater detail, and was not cross-examined. Anthony Joyce described how his dogs aroused him, and he went out and saw the party of six men, whom he followed to his brother John's house, and with his brother and nephew from thence to Michael Casey's house, out of which came the prisoner, Patrick Casey, of Derry, and three others. They then traced the ten men to Joyce's house.

Cross-examined by Mr. Malley—When he saw the six men first he thought they were going to his brother's house, and that was why he followed them. Shortly after the ten men left Michael Casey's house to go towards Joyce's, he and his brother and nephew were not far behind them. He could hear the noise of tongues as if they were talking. Three tenants live between witness and the prisoner's house. Pat Joyce, who was convicted in the previous case, was one of those tenants.

To Mr. Justice Barry—It was about breakfast hour on the 18th of August that he heard the Joyces had been murdered.

Re-examined by Mr. Murphy—He then went and saw the murdered family, and returned to the house of his brother John, where there was a conversation about the murder in presence of John's daughter.

Mr. Murphy proposed to ask what was said, but Mr. Malley objected, and his lordship did not allow the evidence.

The court, at the conclusion of the witness's evidence adjourned till ten o'clock this morning.

FOURTH DAY.

(Abridged from "Freeman" of November 17).

FURTHER DISCLOSURES.

Yesterday, shortly after ten o'clock, the trial of Patrick Casey, for the wilful murder, on the morning of the 18th August, of Bridget Joyce, wife of John Joyce, of Maamtrasna, was resumed.

One of the informers gave very important evidence, which was novel in almost its entirety. Before his examination an incident occurred in which he was concerned. After he was called the learned judge retired from the bench for a few moments. The witness stood upon the steps of the witness table near the dock, and the eyes of the prisoner and of the witness met. The prisoner shook his head, and the witness thereupon retired to a seat under the galleries, followed by the prisoner's eyes. The informer in his evidence disclosed the names of two persons not in custody, who, he said, were the authors of the expedition.

Constable Johnson was permitted by the Court to be recalled by the Attorney-General, in reply to whom he stated that on the night of the murder of the Joyces he was out on patrol about two miles from the scene of the murder. He produced certain bullets which he had found in the house of the murdered family.

Cross-examined by Mr. Malley—I was patrolling in the direction of Finney, which is separated from the scene of the murder by a mountain. I was on the Clonbur side of Finney, which is the side most remote from the Joyces' house.

John Joyce, of Derry, brother of Anthony Joyce, who was examined on the previous evening, deposed to being aroused on the night of the 17th August by Anthony, who lived a short distance from him, and to their going out, with witness's son, to see the six men whom Anthony had observed on the road. He witnessed the six men going into Michael Casey's house, which is some distance beyond his own house. When ten men came out of Michael Casey's house, and came round by the back of that house into a boreen, witness and his son and brother were under a bush behind Michael Casey's house. Witness named the ten men who came out of Michael Casey's house. The prisoner Patrick Casey was one of those men. He had known the ten men a long time, and the prisoner he had known since he (the prisoner) was a little boy. Witness and his companions remained at the bush until they saw at what side the ten men would turn. The men passed into a boreen and kept along it until they went as far as the schoolhouse. Witness and his companions followed them through the boreen. When the ten men reached the schoolhouse they turned to the left and went down into a hollow, making straight to Maamtrasna. Witness still followed. The ten men crossed the river Strangalone and made up the mountain towards the house of John Joyce. The ten men kept to the right. Witness and his companions struck up the mountain after them, keeping some distance to their left. Witness and his son and Anthony went to a corner of the yard and concealed themselves behind a little bush. [The plans were exhibited, and showed that the yard is surrounded by a low wall. In the centre of the yard, and in front of the dwellinghouse, there is a cowhouse. The bush is inside the wall, in the corner farthest from the boreen, which ran alongside one gable of the dwellinghouse. A stile in the wall at the end of which stands the little bush gives an opening from that side into the yard. The line of vision lies obliquely from the bush to the door of the dwellinghouse, and past the side of the cowhouse, so closely that if the cowhouse were a little nearer the bush it would have obscured the witness's view of the dwellinghouse door.] Witness and his companions saw the ten men go into the yard. They made a drive at the door. Some went into the house and some remained outside. Witness heard strong voices calling and screeching from the house.

Cross-examined—Witness said he certainly was asleep when Anthony came to the door, and was awakened by Anthony calling from outside. He heard Anthony calling plainly. Without waiting to dress himself he let Anthony in; he then called up his son Patrick, put on his trousers, waistcoat, and hat, and dressed merely in that manner went out with his son Patrick, and Anthony, who was also without his coat. Witness was a short distance in advance of the ten men when the latter came out of Michael Casey's house. He was a very short distance from them, and saw them clearly, but he could not state who among the ten left Casey's house first or last. When witness and his companions and the party of ten men were going up the hill from the river to John Joyce's house the party could have seen witness had there not been a little hillock around which witness and his son and Anthony went. The ten men were at Joyce's house before witness. There was a stile near the yard—a pretty high stile—and he could see the men crossing it, but he could not say which of the ten went over the stile first; they went up one after the other.

Mr Justice Barry—You say you were before the ten men who left Michael Casey's house. What, then, prevented the ten men seeing you when they came out of Casey's house.

Witness—The shade of the wall and the bush.

A Juror, with a view to ascertain if witness could judge of distance, asked him if he had ever seen a milestone?

Witness—There is no such thing near me (laughter).

Mr. Malley—Is there not a fine country road to Maamtrasna?

Witness—There is.

Mr. Murphy—And what does that prove?

Mr. Malley—I will tell you what it proves by and by.

Patrick Joyce, son of last witness, deposed that his mother and his sister Mary and another sister were in the house when his uncle Anthony came. He had a conversation with his uncle Anthony and his father before they left the house. The bush at which they stood to watch the ten men coming out of Michael Casey's house was at the back of the house, and at the corner of the boreen. While he was standing behind this bush the ten men passed in front and quite close to them into the boreen. They passed so close that he was able to know all the men except one. Patrick Casey, the prisoner, was in the party. Casey lives in the house next to witness, and witness had known him all his life. As the ten men passed into the boreen they were talking, but witness could not understand a word they said. The ten men passed along the back of Thomas Joyce's house.

Cross-examined—We did not leave the bush until the ten men had gone so far that we thought they could not see us. We then followed them, but whenever we came too close to them we stood to allow them to go on a little. We never let them out of sight. We saw no one else join those ten men along the road; I do not believe any other men could have joined them without my seeing them.

Could any man have left the party along the road before they reached Joyce's house? The ten we saw first were the ten we saw go into the yard of Joyce's house. The place at which we were nearest to the ten men was the bush at Casey's house; the place we were next nearest, was the bush at John Joyce's house.

Mary Joyce, sister of last witness, deposed to her father, brother, and uncle Anthony, leaving the house, and to their return before daybreak.

Anthony Philbin, one of the approvers, deposed that on the evening before the murder he met his brother-in-law, Tom Casey, of Glensaul. Casey asked him to accompany him to Derry, and he did so. On the way they met Patrick Joyce and his son Tom and Myles Joyce, who had come out of the fields to them. They were then five in number. A short time afterwards Martin Joyce joined them, having come out of another field. The six of them then went towards Michael Casey's house. Witness turned into Casey's yard and allowed the other five to go into the house. They remained in the house ten or twelve minutes; and when witness, after they came out, rejoined the party on the road, under Casey's house, it numbered nine men. The additional four men were—Patrick Joyce, who was tried yesterday; Patrick Casey, the present prisoner; Michael Casey, the owner of the house—an old man, and John Casey. Witness was the hindmost man of the party, and went wherever the others went. He did not know the country; he was not there previously for sixteen years, when he attended a burial. He did not notice any others join the party before they reached the house of John Joyce; he did not then know to whom the house belonged. Some of the party were talking as they went along towards Joyce's house, but he had not much discourse with them. He saw Patrick Joyce (who was convicted yesterday), Patrick Casey (the prisoner), and Myles Joyce going up to John Joyce's house, run against it, and shove it in, and then enter the house. He heard screeches and a shot. He was only four or five yards away. There were some men between him and the door when it was being broken in, and they moved up the yard, and when the shot was fired there was no one between him and the door.

To a Juror witness said after the shot he ran home as fast as he could to Cappaduff. It was about five or six miles from Maamtrasna, and he was home before daybreak. He lived in the centre of the village of Cappaduff.

Witness was cross-examined by Mr. Malley as to his having left his house at nightfall on the night of the murder before he met his brother-in-law. He explained that a road runs from the village to his land, and that each evening the neighbours' cows trespass upon his lands, and that was why he went out. In his district the cows come home every evening in summer, because there is not sufficient grazing on the mountains for the cows to be left out at night. He could not tell which of the men came first out of Michael Casey's house, nor did he see anything particular about the place, because he was not looking about him. The nine men were getting into a field; when he rejoined them at John Joyce's house, the men went across the style as fast as they could. The man before me was taking his legs over the top of the stile as witness was beginning to ascend it. The door was open after the men entered the house, but he could not see into the house to know what they were doing, the place was so dark. While he remained in the yard none of the party went into the house except the three he had mentioned.

To a Juror, witness said that on his return home he did not pass Michael Casey's house. He did not know what route he took. He believed he crossed a stream. He did not want to go near any house or any person. His desire was to get home as fast as he could. When he joined the party he did not know what they were "on" for.

Thomas Casey (the second approver), brother-in-law of Philbin, the first approver, and residing at Glensaul, was next examined. He was repeatedly directed by the Attorney-General to keep his eyes raised to the jury, and jurors several times requested him to speak louder. He had known the prisoner, he said, for 15 years.

The Attorney-General—Immediately before the murder did the prisoner give you any instructions? He did.

Tell the jury what the prisoner said to you? The night before the murder——

Mr. Malley objected to the evidence but the objection was overruled.

Witness—On the night before the murder he told me to go towards Derry. He told me I had to go there, and to bring Anthony Philbin with me.

To bring him where? He told me to bring him along with me.

I know; but where were you to bring Philbin to? To go towards Derry to meet the rest of them. He didn't tell me exactly where to go to but that I had to go, and that I would see them.

Would see who—tell the jury the exact words the prisoner used? That is all he told me, that I had to go.

Who did he mean by "them"—that you would see "them?" He did not mention their names.

What did you understand him to mean? I understood him to mean that I should go as far as Michael Casey's house.

A Juror—You have repeated two or three times that you had to go. Were you compelled to go?

Witness—Well, it seemed so from the way he told me to go.

To the Attorney-General—I was working in the bog when the prisoner came to me and told me I had to go. It was in the evening. He seemed to have come from his own home at Derry to me. I do not believe I ever had seen John Joyce before the murder, but I heard of him before it.

Had you any conversation with the prisoner about John Joyce before that night? We were talking about him at the fair of Toormakeady—it was held on SS. Peter and Paul's day (June 29th).

What did the prisoner say to you about him? He said he believed that there was something going to be done to him. He did not mention what it was. He did not seem to know.

Did he say why anything was to be done to him? He did not.

Mr. Justice Barry—The prisoner, you say, did not appear to know what it was?

Witness—I cannot say about that.

The Attorney-General—Did you ask the prisoner what was to be done to John Joyce?

Witness—I did not.

Did you see the prisoner again after that? I saw him again at Mass, and was talking to him. But the conversation was not about that affair—the murder of John Joyce affair.

A Juror—What word was that which the witness has used?

The Attorney-General and the learned judge concurred in saying that they thought the expression "the murder of John Joyce affair" was only a descriptive expression by the witness.

The witness, in reply to further questions from the Attorney-General, said that he did not "witness" that he met the prisoner except at Mass. When he started from Cappaduff on the evening of the murder he cut through the mountains and came to Philbin's house.

Did you tell Philbin what Casey had told you? I told him that I had been told he had to come with me. I do not think I mentioned Casey's name to him.

Tell the jury what words you used to Philbin. I told Philbin that I had been sent that direction.

Mr. Justice Barry—Did you say you and Philbin had to go?

Witness—Yes, I said we had to go.

A Juror—Was Philbin expecting you before you went to him? I do not know about that.

The Attorney-General—When you gave Philbin the message did you both start to go towards Derry?

Witness—Yes, we took the shortest route we could towards Derry.

Did you meet with any other men? Yes. When we got close to Derry we met the three Joyces. They were close to the house—Patrick Joyce, Tom Joyce, and Myles Joyce.

Did they join you, or you join them? We joined them, and we all went on together. Martin Joyce immediately after came to us from out of a garden. He joined our party also. We went on together towards Michael Casey's house at Derry.

[The Attorney-General here directed the witness to remove his eyes from him, and to look upon the jury.]

On further examination, the witness said the most of the party went into Michael Casey's house. The Joyces all went in. He himself stood in the doorway.

Did any of you stay outside? I do not know whether Philbin stayed outside or went in. Pat Casey (the prisoner at the bar), and Michael Casey, and Tom Casey were at this house when we arrived.

Were they all dressed in the house? They were sitting and standing about the house. I do not remember if the man of the house, Michael Casey, was dressed. The prisoner said nothing to me in the house. They may have had some conversation among themselves, but I did not overhear it, because I went outside the door. I cannot exactly bring to recollection how long the party remained in the house. They were more than a few minutes. It was late at night; I think it was near midnight, but I cannot say what time it was. The whole party came out together. The prisoner was in the party. He was my companion along the way, but we did not say much to each other. I cannot give an account now of what we said. I know that part of the country; I went to it at different times before, but it was not at night. After we left the Caseys' house we kept on the boreen, I cannot tell for how far we kept upon it. At times we went through fields. [The witness was directed to speak louder.] In the end the entire party of ten men came to John Joyce's house at Maamtrasna. We were joined some time before we reached John Joyce's house by two additional men—Patrick Kelly and Michael Nee. The latter I knew well. He was a pedlar at one time, and two years before this I got a revolver from him to keep, which I returned to him shortly afterwards. I did not know Kelly. I have not seen either Kelly or Nee since the night of the murder.

To the Jury—It was a short time before we crossed the river that these two additional men joined us. They came to us over a wall from a field, and seemed to me to have been waiting for us.

The Attorney-General—Did they appear to be known to any of the men in the party?

Witness—Nee came and spoke to me directly after he joined us. Both Nee and Kelly spoke to the prisoner and Pat Joyce. Nee told me that the second man was Patrick Kelly. The two men continued with us, and were the first that went into the yard of John Joyce's house. They went in first along with the three whom I afterwards saw at the door. [The witness was again directed to speak louder].

Who were the three? Patrick Joyce, Myles Joyce, and Patrick Casey (the prisoner), and Patrick Kelly, and Michael Nee. The five went to the door. They pushed it in. I was standing at the gable end of the cowhouse, or barn, at the time. I cannot say if the five men went into the house, because it was dark; but after the door was pushed in I did not see the five men, and I knew the rest were standing about the yard. Immediately after they went in I heard a few words of talk, then a shout, and then a shot. I was not able to distinguish what was said. There were a good many reports of shots in the house. I remained in the yard until I noticed some of the men coming out, and I then made off.

Who did you see come out? I cannot say who came out first. I cannot say if the five came out. I noticed some men in the door coming out, and then I made off towards my own house at Glensaul. I got home about daylight. I saw a party coming after me, but I always kept my distance. They were not pursuing me.

The Attorney-General proposed to ask what communication Nee made to witness when he joined the party, but his lordship did not think the question could he put.

Cross-examined by Mr. Stritch—In consequence of the darkness I could not see whether the prisoner went into the house. I took no notice of any stile, and I jumped into the yard from the wall beside the boreen (which would be the wall farthest from the bush).

Did you or did you not know that you were going to do anything wrong to John Joyce that night? I did not know what they were going to do to him.

Had you any suspicion? Well, I wont say anything about that, because I do not know.

Do you expect the jury to believe that? I cannot help that. Can you make me tell the truth—

Mr. Stritch—I don't expect I can.

Witness—And then make me eat it. Do you want me to compose it all over again and to tell a lie.

And if you had known it was to kill Joyce would you have given him warning? Indeed I would not.

Would you have told the police? I would not. I did not want to interfere.

You kept the secret locked up in your breast from the 29th June until the present? I did not know anything that was going to take place. I was speaking with Philbin while we were in custody. I first heard last week that he would give evidence for the Crown. I did not hear that his life would be saved on that account—that was in the honour of the Crown to do it.

Did that influence you to give evidence also to save your life? I do not know whether it will be done or not.

Would you give the information for the purpose of saving your neck? That is not a fair question (laughter).

The Attorney-General rebuked any spirit of levity being shown in so serious a case.

The Witness—If you were dragged into a " hole of water " by two or three men maybe you would sooner be out of it than stay there.

Mr. Stritch—Is it to save your life that you are giving this evidence? I would like to save my life, and so would everybody.

Answer me " Yes" or " No?" I won't answer you.

Have you told us now about the other two men? Why wouldn't I tell about Kelly and Nee, because I knew they were the authors of it (excitement in court).

The Attorney-General—Now we have got it out. There is the root of the confederacy.

Mr. Stritch (to witness)—How do you know that?

Witness—By the way Nee was talking.

To the Attorney-General—Kelly was a stranger in that district. I don't recollect seeing him before that night.

To Mr. Stritch—I knew he was not a policeman when I saw him.

Sub-Inspector Philips, Mr. Gardiner, R.M., and Dr. Ingham then gave formal evidence.

Mr. O'Malley opened the defence.

Mary Casey, a young woman, cousin of the prisoner, living at Shanvallycahill, a quarter of a mile from the prisoner's residence, deposed (in Irish), in reply to Mr. Stritch, that she remembered the day before the murder of the Joyces. She went on the morning of that day to the prisoner's house. His mother and the prisoner and herself were the only occupants of the house. The prisoner had been making a barn during the day, and when he came in at evening complained of a pain in his stomach. She and his mother sat up all night warming milk for him. From the time Patrick Casey entered the house in the evening he did not leave it until breakfast time next morning.

Cross-examined by the Attorney-General—She earned her livelihood by her day's pay, and she went to the prisoner's house on the day in question to spin wool for an obligation. She had worked there every day since for half her time. She was surprised when she heard of Patrick Casey's arrest.

Miss Julia Casey, mother of the prisoner, examined through the interpreter, corroborated the testimony of last witness. She added that for a week before the murder the prisoner did not leave the house at night. She heard of the murder about the middle of the day after it occurred.

Cross-examined by Mr. Murphy—She said her son was well of the pain by daylight on the morning after the murder, and went out to clump turf as usual, and came home to breakfast. He got better about breakfast time.

Mr. Murphy—I thought she said he went out before breakfast time?

The Interpreter—She says now it was after breakfast.

Mr. Murphy (to interpreter)—Did you interpret her evidence correctly when you said she first stated he went out to work and came back to breakfast?

Interpreter—I did.

The witness added that the persons at work with her son on the day of the murder and the day after were John Casey, Matthias Casey, John Joyce, and the boy. Witness heard of the murder from people who were going to the corps' house—the house where the Joyces were murdered.

Mr. Ryan was re-called by Mr. Stritch, and stated that the bush at John Joyce's house was 57 feet from the dwellinghouse door.

Mr. Stritch addressed the court for the prisoner.

Mr. Murphy, Q.C., replied for the Crown.

At the close of the learned counsel's address there was applause in court.

Mr. Justice Barry suggested, it being then so late (a quarter to six) that the case could not close to-night. It would be better, for reasons which he might not particularise, that they should leave over till next day the conclusion of the case.

The jury concurred, and at their suggestion the Court decided to resume at ten o'clock this morning.

FIFTH DAY.

CONVICTION AND SENTENCE OF PATRICK CASEY.

(Abridged from " Freeman " of November 18).

Yesterday, shortly after ten o'clock, the trial of Patrick Casey (which commenced on Wednesday afternoon) for the murder of Bridget Joyce, wife of John Joyce, of Maamtrasna, on the 17th of August, was resumed.

Mr. Justice Barry, on taking his seat on the bench, proceeded to address the jury.

The jury retired to consider their verdict at twelve minutes past eleven o'clock. The learned judge thereupon retired from the bench, and the prisoner was removed from the dock. At twenty-four minutes past eleven, after an absence of twelve minutes, the jury returned to their box.

The prisoner was again brought into the dock, and he stood before the bar without any emotion or excitement visible in the features of his face.

The learned judge having been communicated with, came into court, after an interval of a few moments.

The Foreman of the jury handed down the issue paper, and in reply to the Clerk of the Crown, stated that they had agreed to their verdict, and that that verdict was

GUILTY.

The prisoner stood looking at the bench without a tremor, as if his face had been petrified. After a few minutes he raised his eyes to the jury-box, then looked around the court. His apparent stolidness seemed to indicate not so much indifference to his dreadful position as an ignorance of the character of the verdict of the jury.

The Clerk of the Crown, in the language formally prescribed, informed him of the verdict of his country.

The prisoner replied with a puzzled expression of face, "I do not understand a word you are saying," and looked around the court as if for the interpreter.

The Clerk of the Crown (continuing the formal address) asked if he had anything to say why sentence of death and execution should not be awarded against him,

The Prisoner—I have to say that I had nothing at all to do with it.

The Court, thinking he was requesting the services of the interpreter directed the interpreter to communicate to him the fact that the Court now called upon him to say why sentence of death should not be passed upon him.

The Interpreter went to the dock and commenced to make the communication in English, but the prisoner, being in an attitude of the greatest attention, requested him to speak in Irish.

The Interpreter did so, and the prisoner seemed dumbfounded by the communication, but after a moment or two responded in Irish.

The Interpreter—He says, my lord, "I have nothing to say; but I will say this, whatever happens to me, that I had no hand in it."

[The following address of the judge, in passing sentence, was delivered in presence of the jurors who were waiting to try Myles Joyce, the third prisoner, whose trial commenced within a few minutes after this address:—]

Mr. Justice Barry, in passing sentence, said—

Patrick Casey, after a most patient trial, you have been convicted by a jury of your fellow-countrymen of the crime of murder. The murder charged against you, in the indictment of which you have been convicted, is the murder of Bridget Joyce. But the evidence has established clearly and conclusively, and so as not to leave a doubt of your guilt upon the mind of any sane person who has heard or read that evidence, that you not only murdered Bridget Joyce, but four other persons on that one occasion. Enormous as the crime is, its enormity seems to sink into insignificance before the singular mystery which surrounds it. It appears upon the evidence, clearly and distinctly, that the dreadful deed was committed in pursuance of orders issued by some unseen or unknown tribunal or man. You were the person who conveyed the orders to one person, Thomas Casey. You told him he should go to Derry on the particular night. You told him he should bring his brother-in-law, Anthony Philbin, with him. In obedience to the orders so communicated to him Thomas Casey summoned his brother-in-law, Anthony Philbin, simply telling him he should go. Strange to relate, in conveying those orders, from whomsoever they originally emanated, to his own brother-in-law (Anthony Philbin), Thomas Casey never mentioned the name of the person who conveyed those orders to him. In pursuance of those orders, Thomas Casey and Anthony Philbin attended on that occasion. Strange to relate —dreadful to relate—the family which was to be murdered that night was absolutely unknown to Anthony Philbin. He says he did not know, and probably he did not know, what deed was to be worked upon the family; but that, in that remote, once peaceful district, there should exist such a state of things as this—that two men receive orders (they do not inquire from whom, they are not told from whom) to attend on the particular night, and that they did attend there—whether voluntarily or reluctantly does not matter much—is testified by the eye witnesses and participators of the deed of carnage which has shocked civilised humanity. Such was the deed ; such were the circumstances under which you committed the deed.

As I have said on a recent occasion, vile as a criminal may be, I discharge with pain the duty of pronouncing the doom of death against my fellow-man. [His lordship exhibited considerable emotion.] But if ever there was a case in which a man's repugnance ought to be overcome, or could be overcome, if ever there was a case in which combined sense of horror at the crime and necessity of duty ought steel a man's nerves against emotion or distress, that case is the present. I shall add no words to attempt to make you feel conscious of the position in which you stand. You have no mercy to expect in this world. I ask you to turn to that God whose dictates and precepts you have so dreadfully disobeyed. It only remains for me now to pronounce upon you that dreadful sentence which it is my duty to pronounce. [Assuming the black cap, the learned judge pronounced, in the usual formal language, that the prisoner be hung at Galway Jail on the 15th December next.]

The condemned man stood motionless in the dock for a little while, then took his cap from the seat beside him and beckoned the interpreter to come near. He whispered to the interpreter, who informed the court that the prisoner had asked "What day?" The unfortunate man was informed the 15th December, and he, looking upwards, with a most reverent and touching aspect, exclaimed, in the Irish language, "I have expectation of heaven." He then followed the warder to the cells beneath the court.

TRIAL OF MYLES JOYCE.

The third prisoner, Myles Joyce, was, before a quarter of an hour had elapsed, brought into the dock to stand his trial for complicity in the murder. The prisoner is older than either of the previous men who have been tried. He was dressed in older garments, but, unlike them, he did not appear to have the slightest knowledge of the language in which his trial is being conducted.' He sits in the dock like them, and like the young man Patrick Walsh, who was recently convicted of the murder of Constable Kavanagh, with his head leaning upon his arms, which he rests upon the bar of the dock.

The jury which served in the preceding case was discharged by the learned judge.

The long panel was called over on fines of £20.

Mr. Malley, Q.C., then rose and said—My lord, it becomes my imperative duty to apply to your lordship that the trial of the prisoner who now stands at the bar be postponed, under the circumstances which I am about to mention to your lordship. I move, upon the affidavit of Mr. Henry Concannon, solicitor for the prisoner, who says:—

"I, Henry Concannon, make oath and say that I am the solicitor acting for the defence of the traversers yet on trial for the murder of the Joyce family at Maamtrasna on the 18th August last. That from its awful nature the crime absorbed the attention of the public and excited an universal indignation and a fierce desire to bring the perpetrators to speedy punishment. That the case has since the opening of the present Commission, on the 25th day of October last, been kept prominently before the public, and the horrible details of the crime have been frequently published before the trials in the newspapers circulating among the jurors of the city and county of Dublin, by whom the cases are to be tried. That on the 1st day of November the accused were called on to plead, and the hearing of the trial was then fixed for Monday, the 13th inst. That immediately before the trial two of the traversers offered to give evidence to criminate the other traversers, and disclosed details which I, as traverser's solicitor, was wholly unacquainted with, and which took their counsel completely by surprise. That the necessary result of the foregoing matter has been to create, develop, and sustain a fierce public indignation, and to direct all its force against the accused. That on the verdict being made public in the case of Patrick Joyce, the comments thereon in the public Press of this city are calculated to render an impartial unprejudiced trial of the cause impossible for some time to come."

I need not mention to your lordship that it is a proud boast of this country that every subject of the realm when called upon to stand his trial for his life, is entitled as of right and by sanction of the Constitution under which we live, to the fairest and most impartial trial. But if this wretched Irish-speaking creature, who has never had the advantage of education, and who will be unable to understand the language in which his accusers will give their evidence, or the language in which the counsel against him will arraign him or your lordship address the jury—if the trial of this wretched creature, be brought on now under the circumstances which are referred to in this affidavit, who can say that the proud boast of our Constitution will be maintained in this instance? My lord, illiterate the prisoner is and incapable of instructing us, and I cannot but say that I feel embarrassed to the extremest extent. There have been two trials. Your lordship has heard the evidence and noted it attentively, and your lordship has just recapitulated that evidence on the second occasion, and shown the jury that it was almost the same as in the first. Your lordship, in terms which could not but be approved by every person who heard them, sentenced the last prisoner to death, and in doing so your lordship necessarily referred to the fact that the evidence laid against the prisoner was cogent and conclusive. This, the third man, is about to be put upon his trial in the presence of this court, and perhaps to be tried by jurors who were sitting in this court when the two former trials took place, who heard all the evidence, and who listened to the observations of your lordship. A jury is about to be empannelled to give a verdict in this case according to the evidence which has been twice repeated, and which is a third time to be deposed to. It is a fearful responsibility for any counsel to undertake to stand up here, before this court, and before a jury empanelled under conditions I have described, and to strive to distinguish, after what has fallen from your lordship's lips, the evidence which now may be adduced; and to prove to a third jury that the prisoner who is arraigned for the same offence is clearly entitled to a verdict of not guilty. My lord, in a criminal case, when a counsel accepts the responsibility which is imposed upon him he cannot as in a civil case retire from it even if he would, and, my lord, if your lordship will not grant the postponement which I humbly ask, it will be necessary for me immediately after the effects which were produced at these two trials, and ere these effects have been effaced, to perform my duty. I cannot say it is an agreeable duty—it will be necessary for me to stand up in this court, and to exercise to the best of my ability in the defence of this unfortunate man. I submit, my lord, that the circumstances deposed to in this affidavit are sufficient to show that a strong case has been made out why this man and his advisers should get some little time to prepare for a trial which as yet, I must say, has mystery about it. The evidence given by the two approvers goes to show, and I know not how it is, that there is some one who has given, as it was called, " orders." My lord, I know not to what extent ——

The Attorney-General—My learned friend will pardon me, but I do not think it is open to him to comment in anticipation upon the evidence which will be given or to comment either upon the evidence which has been given in a past trial.

Mr Malley—I am commenting upon this paragraph in the affidavit—" That immediately before the trial, two of the traversers offered to give evidence to criminate the other traversers, and disclosed details which I, as traversers' solicitor, was wholly unacquainted with, and which took their counsel completely by surprise." Does not that open to me the right to refer to the evidence now in the recollection of your lordship. I am sorry that the Attorney-General should object to my referring to that which is in our immediate recollection. I only referred to it for the purpose of saying that if the mystery be explored it may throw additional light upon the case before your lordship. I intended saying no more when the Attorney-General interposed. I am sure the Attorney-General will, with the fairness which has marked his conduct of these cases, admit that that is not too far to go. I submit it is necessary for the justice, and certainly would be merciful, at least, to this poor man, that my application should be acceded to.

The Attorney-General—My lord, it is my duty, on the part of the Crown, to oppose any such motion. We cannot doubt that the prisoners so far have received the fairest and most impartial trial ; that the evidence adduced was most carefully considered by the jury ; and, I shall take leave to say, put by the bench in a manner which made it perfectly transparent to the jury. So far as I myself and my learned colleagues in this case are concerned, I think I need only appeal to the bench for confirmation of the statement that the fairest way in which men could be put upon their trial, where a number of persons are concerned, is one by one, so as to individualise the evidence against each, and to prevent the evidence which might be given against all, but could not be given against one, being offered against all the accused. The other point relied on was comments in the public Press. I am glad to take this opportunity for saying that in my humble opinion—it is of course entitled to no particular weight—the conduct of the public Press has been perfectly exemplary in this case. Nothing has been done to inflame public opinion ; nothing has been done—at least so far as has come under my notice—to prejudice the trial of the prisoner. I think the Press has set an example which, on this occasion, deserves the highest commendation. With reference to any comments upon myself. I, of course, say nothing. The last ground relied on is that the evidence in the last two trials must be given also in this case ; that that evidence has been matter of public consideration, and possibly has been weighed by jurors in court who will be called in this case. That is a ground which I submit cannot be entertained. My learned friend says it entitles him to say that no fair trial of the prisoner can be had for a considerable time. It is impossible to entertain a ground of that kind, because no length of the time which could be allowed to elapse would obliterate the evidence from the public mind. No matter at what distance of time from this the accused are separately put upon their trial, the same evidence must be given. The conduct of the jurors in the past gives your lordship and the public the greatest confidence in the jurors who will be called upon to try this case. I must say, further, it is not the case that the two prisoners who supplied information gave it before the trials commenced. One prisoner did so before the trial commenced, and as soon as the Crown was in possession of the fact, a note of the evidence was furnished to the other side. The other prisoner gave information while the trial was proceeding, and on the same day, and as rapidly as possible, information was given to the other side. No ground has been put forward for acceding to the motion of my learned friend.

Mr. Murphy—My learned friend (Mr. Malley) says it is possible there may be some elucidation of this mysterious affair—namely, from whom the orders originated—if an adjournment be granted. Possibly there might ; but what assistance would such an elucidation give to the defence of the prisoner now on trial. It is necessary that the investigation of a crime should follow as soon as possible after the event. We do not know what may take place with respect to any of those witnesses if the trial were postponed. We do not know what calamity might happen which would prevent these men coming forward and giving the evidence which they are ready to give now. There can be no reason given for the postponement of this trial except that the account of a certain transaction which has been already investigated as to one person has been given in public court. That must occur in the cases of all persons where only one is put forward on trial at a time. We might have put forward three of the prisoners together, or any two, or any four of them. The Attorney-General considering that they might possibly be embarrassed by such a course, took the present much fairer course. A third prisoner has now been put upon his trial. If the evidence which has been heard, and which will be heard again, is too cogent, or too clear, or too irrefutable, that is not a reason, why this case should be postponed. On the contrary I submit it is a reason why the case should be at once investigated.

Mr. Stritch—It is not on the ground of the evidence being too cogent we seek a postponement, but because of the difficulty we have in defending new prisoners on the same evidence before the same tribunal, when scarcely any person in court has not heard that evidence. There has been great excitement in court, comments have appeared in the public Press. We do not complain of these comments; on the contrary, Mr. Malley and myself are prepared to endorse everything which has been said by the Attorney-General regarding the Press. But there is no doubt that all the newspapers have published detailed accounts of the shocking crime which occurred at Maamtrasna, and while these comments are fresh in the minds of the people, the difficulty of our defending the remaining prisoners are far above the inconvenience which might arise from an adjournment of the trial. We only seek a postponement for the purpose of securing a fair and better opportunity of defending the prisoner. The effect of elucidating the case might be to clear the prisoner or all of them. We wish to have for this prisoner a tribunal in which judgment shall not have been given against us already.

Mr. Justice Barry—I should certainly be always very willing to accede to any application the object of which was to secure that which it is my duty to secure to every man brought before me—a fair and impartial trial, and which, with the blessing of God, I shall, as long as I occupy the seat which I now occupy, endeavour to secure for every man arraigned before me. But I have also to consider the duty imposed upon me of maintaining the regularity of our procedure and the due course of the administration of the law. It would be introducing a very dangerous precedent indeed if I acceded to this application for postponement on grounds so vague and unsubstantial as are put forward in the affidavit of Mr. Concannon. If any newspapers had been produced before me containing comments calculated to prejudice the fair trial of this case, whether the fair trial was to the prejudice of or in favour of the prisoner, I would know very well how to deal with the case as well as with the publishers of such comments. No such newspaper has been produced; and I am asked in fact to postpone this case on the ground that newspapers were published which Mr. Stritch in his reply admits contained nothing of an objectionable character. As regards the surprise, that was the ground of an application made before, and which was disposed of by me. I might go much more into detail if I were sitting in chamber, and not in open court, as to the reasons for which I refuse this application; but as that might involve more or less the discussion of matters which I do not care to be the person to introduce, I think it is better not to refer to them. I do not mean to convey that I have any opinions with regard to the case—I mean grounds of a legal character which I should address to the counsel engaged. I adopt the same rule as is followed in civil cases on applications for new trials, simply to refuse the motion or grant the motion without any comment. Comment upon the matters alluded to in the affidavit of the prisoner might lead to consequences which I should deplore, and consequently I best discharge my duty.—best in every sense of the word—by simply saying I consider the grounds put forward insufficient to warrant me in granting the postponement.

The prisoner at the bar was then informed, through the interpreter, that a jury was about to be sworn to try him, and also that he had a right to challenge twenty, and as many more as he could show cause for. The prisoner listened attentively, but made no reply.

The following gentlemen were ordered by the Crown to stand by :— Daniel Toole, Henry street; Edward Malone, Lucan; Francis Caher, Mulhuddert; Andrew Thompson, Ormond quay; Michael O'Reilly, Thomas street; Thomas Kelly, Rathcoole; James M'Donnell, Britain street;

Richard O'Mally, Santry ; Patrick Nowlan, Golden Bawn ; Patk. Gordon, Middle Abbey street ; Luke F. O'Reilly, Middle Abbey street ; Frederick Keightley, Westland row ; Wm. Pillar, Camden street ; Michael Hayden, George's street ; Joseph Fitzpatrick, Swords ; Hugh O'Donnell, Queen street ; John Carver, Earl street ; George Hickson, Kingstown ; D. Sherwin, Naul ; Michael Caher, Clonsilla ; Peter M'Cready, Belview ; James Dollard, Strand street ; Daniel Geoghegan, Kingstown ; Richard Ward, Townsend street ; Wm. Carey, Baggot street ; Michael Becker, George's street, south ; John Harris, Dawson street.

The following challenges were made for the prisoner :—
James Robertson, Dawson street ; Henry T. Arnott, Ormond quay ; William R. Jones, Monkstown ; Frederick Maunders, Simmons court ; Frederick Thompson, Breffni terrace ; Launcelot G. Watson, Blackrock ; William M. Battersby, Westmoreland street ; William Scale, Grafton street ; John Gibbs, Pembroke road ; Hamilton D. Athol, Upper Sackville street ; Joseph Lewers, Sackville street ; William Carter, Poolbeg street ; William Perrin, Northumberland road ; Charles A. Bayley, Finglas ; Henry T. Dockrell, Kingstown (who was also ordered to stand aside, but the prisoner having challenged first, it was counted against him).

During the swearing of the jury Andrew Fitzpatrick, of Nassau-street, was challenged for the prisoner on cause shown.

Mr. Malley proposed to make the challenge on *irvo dire* for the purpose of questioning the juror, and quoted in support of his contention that he could do so, the case of the Queen *v* Mary M'Mahon.

Mr. Justice Barry said there was no question of challenge in that case. It did not lay down that when a gentleman came to take the book for the purpose of being sworn, and before the challenge was handed in counsel had a right to cross-examine him regarding his opinions. That was not the law.

Mr. Malley thereupon handed in the necessary form of challenge, setting forth on parchment that Andrew Fitzpatrick did " not stand indifferently between our said lady the Queen and the prisoner at the bar."

A ballot was made for two gentlemen to try the allegation, and Mr. James Shiel, of Rathcoole, and Mr. Richard Pigott, of Kingstown, were chosen.

Mr. Fitzpatrick, examined by Mr. Malley, said he was in court for a short time during the previous trial. He was not acquainted with the details, and had not formed any opinion on the case, indeed he had conscientiously abstained from reading the newspaper reports of the trial, because he was on the panel.

The triers accordingly found a verdict that Mr. Fitzpatrick did stand indifferently between the prosecution and the prisoner, and he was sworn as foreman.

The following jury was then sworn :—
Andrew Fitzpatrick, Nassau-street (foreman), Protestant ; Thomas Harper, Naul, Protestant ; Torrence F. M'Cullagh, Abbey-street, Protestant ; Peter Aungier, St. Dolough's, Catholic ; James N. Davis, Rathfarnham Park, Protestant ; Henry Carleton, Eustace-street, Protestant ; William A. Roberts, Grand Canal-street (affirmed), Protestant ; Charles W. Harrison, Brunswick-street, Protestant ; Frederick William Pim, William-street (affirmed), Protestant ; Simon Tracey, Westmoreland-street, Protestant ; Thomas J. Thornhill, Pembroke-road, Protestant ; Thomas Sinnot, Kingstown, Catholic.

The prisoner, Myles Joyce, was then indicted for the wilful murder, on August 18, at Maamtrasna, of Margaret Joyce, the younger.

The prisoner pleaded not guilty, and is defended by the same counsel as in the preceding cases.

The Attorney-General, in opening the case for the Crown, stated that the accused lived at Cappanacreha. Although that was the third time that he had made a statement of the horrid facts of this murder, he was not

F

ashamed to say that he felt even then a choking motion, which he supposed everybody in court felt also at that moment, and which only an anonymous scribbler outside would be brute enough not to feel.

On resuming after an adjournment for luncheon,

A Juror requested his lordship to sit as late as possible this evening so as to obviate the necessity of being kept from their homes on Sunday.

Mr. Justice Barry said he had already intimated his intention of doing so.

Evidence was then entered upon, the facts deposed to being re-stated.

After Anthony Philbin's evidence, the court adjourned till ten o'clock this morning

SIXTH DAY.

CONVICTION AND SENTENCE OF MYLES JOYCE.

(*Abridged from the " Freeman " of November* 20.)

On Saturday, shortly after ten o'clock, in Green-street Courthouse, the trial of Myles Joyce, aged about 45 years, of Cappanacreha, for the wilful murder of Margaret Joyce, jun., aged 17 years, daughter of John Joyce and Bridget Joyce, of Maamtrasna, was resumed before Mr. Justice Barry. Again there was a large audience in the court, which included many ladies. The prisoner, sitting in a corner of the dock, gave a calm but close attention to the evidence.

At the sitting of the Court,

The Attorney-General asked the learned counsel for the defence if the prisoner understood English.

Mr. Concannon replied that he thought he did not, and that it might be better to have the evidence of the witnesses who speak English interpreted to the prisoner in Irish.

The Interpreter asked the prisoner in Irish if he understood the evidence that was being given in English, and informed the Court that the prisoner replied in the affirmative.

Thomas Casey, the second approver, an English-speaking witness, was then examined by the Attorney-General. It was again found necessary to direct this witness several times to speak louder.

John Collins deposed to having found Michael Joyce alive when he entered the house before sunrise on the morning of the 18th.

A Juror (Mr. Pim) asked if Michael Joyce made any statement to him?

Mr. Justice Barry said that question need not be answered. They already had the statement of the doctor that Michael was raving and unable to make any reliable statement.

Dr. Hegarty stated that Michael Joyce was quite irrational subsequent to the injuries inflicted on him. Margaret Joyce (for whose murder the prisoner is on trial) died from injuries inflicted by some heavy weapon. Her skull was smashed in.

The evidence of Sub-Inspector Philips and Mr. Gardiner, R.M., closed the case for the Crown at half-past eleven.

Mr. Malley then opened the prisoner's defence.

Mr. Murphy replied on behalf of the Crown.

Mr. Justice Barry summed up.

The jury retired at three o'clock. At six minutes past that hour they entered the box and announced a verdict of

GUILTY.

The Clerk of the Crown informed him in the usual language of the result. He listened with a quiet but melancholy expression of face, inclining his head to the right. When the Clerk of the Crown had concluded he still kept his eyes fixed upon the Bench, made no attempt to respond, and seemed like a man who had only the vaguest notion of what was going on. The interpreter, Constable Evans, was called by direction of the learned judge, and he communicated to the prisoner in Irish the fact that he had been found guilty. A change then came upon the prisoner. He showed a little fear, and clutched the bar of the dock, but, looking upwards with a fervent expression and attitude of invocation, spoke in Irish. The interpreter rendered it as follows—He leaves it to God and the Virgin above his head. He had no dealing with it, no more than the person who was never born, nor had he against anyone else. For the last twenty years he had done no harm, and if he had, might he never go to heaven. He was as clear of this as the child yet to be born. He slept in his bed with his wife that night, and he had no knowledge about it whatever. He is quite content with whatever the gentlemen may do to him, but whether he is to be hung or crucified he is as free as he can be.

The above statement was made and interpreted by sentences. It merely conveys the tenor, not the full words of the condemned man, who, in making the protestation, frequently invoked the Son of God. Though exhibiting considerable emotion, the prisoner did not lose his self-control in the slightest degree. The scene was very painful, and it scarcely added to its solemnity to observe the many ladies who were amongst the audience, and the obtrusive manner in which the thronged courthouse gazed with the curiosity of interest, rather than of feeling, upon the condemned and sorrowful-looking man. The prisoner's counsel was much moved by the scene, and the learned judge showed considerable emotional feeling.

His lordship then sentenced the prisoner to be executed in Galway Jail on December 15th, the same day as the two prisoners previously sentenced.

The condemned man, touched on the shoulder by the dock warder, then turned slowly away, and with a step, lingering and sorrowful, and a heavy sigh, with which there was an indistinct exclamation in Irish, audible only to a portion of the courthouse, he descended to the cells.

The jury was then discharged.

THE ARCHBISHOP OF TUAM'S LETTER.

The Lord Lieutenant's Reply to the Letter of the Archbishop of Tuam.

The following is the full text of the communication addressed to his Grace the Archbishop of Tuam by the Under Secretary, in obedience to the directions of his Excellency the Lord Lieutenant:—

"The Castle, Dublin, August 23rd, 1884.

"My Lord Archbishop—I am directed by the Lord Lieutenant to inform your Grace that your letter of the 13th instant, the receipt of which was acknowledged by his Excellency the following day, has received his most careful consideration.

"Before the receipt of your Grace's letter attention had been drawn in the House of Commons to the allegation that Thomas Casey, one of the murderers of the Joyce family at Maamtrasna on the 17th August, 1882, who had been accepted as an informer, and had given evidence on the trial, had made a statement to the effect that the evidence he had given on that occasion was false. Immediately thereupon his Excellency gave instructions that the truth of this statement should be tested in connection with the whole circumstances of the trial, and the subsequent history of the witness himself.

"It is not usual for his Excellency to enter into details in communicating his decision on criminal cases, but the present instance is one of such gravity, and the statements alleged to have been made have attracted so much public attention from your Grace's letter, that he has determined to depart from his usual custom, and to put the circumstances of the case fully before you.

"He has, as your Grace has requested, inquired fully into the allegations now made by the informers. He forwards to your Grace a memorandum prepared under his immediate directions, and which has his entire approval, setting forth the results of that inquiry. From this memorandum your Grace will perceive that there was ample evidence at the trial, given by three unimpeached and independent witnesses, to convict all the prisoners without the evidence of Thomas Casey or Anthony Philbin, and that their recent statements do not shake that testimony, which plainly established that Myles Joyce and the prisoners now undergoing penal servitude were themselves members of the party who participated in, or actually committed, the murders of the Joyce family.

"With regard to the actual commission of the murders, his Excellency would observe that an idea seems to prevail in the minds of some persons that the guilt of murder is only attached to those who actually fire the shot or strike the blow which causes death. Such an erroneous idea on the part of some of the participators in this horrible tragedy may account for their assertion of the innocence of those members of the party who, although they aided and countenanced the murders by their presence, and were, therefore, morally and legally guilty of the crime, may not with their own hands have inflicted the wounds which caused the death of their victims.

"I now come to the other point raised in your Grace's letter. A court of law can only act on the evidence placed before it, and, deplorable as it would have been, had it been shown that it had in this case been misled by he false swearing of perjured witnesses, the matter becomes far more serious when it is alleged that the course of justice was perverted by the action of officers of the Crown. The statement which your Grace says Thomas Casey made amounts to this, viz—'That he was told by the official that unless he swore against Myles Joyce, though innocent, he himself would surely be hanged; that he got twenty minutes for deliberation, and then from terror of death swore as had been suggested to him.'

"This is so serious a charge, striking as it does at the root of all confidence in the administration of the law, that the Lord Lieutenant has strictly inquired into the matter to see if the allegation has any colour of foundation—an allegation which no man should lightly entertain on the unsupported assertion of witnesses who aver themselves to have been perjured.

"The communications which took place with Thomas Casey, when he had volunteered to give evidence, and was accepted as an informer, are fully detailed in the memorandum which accompanies this letter. His Excellency has no doubt, after the careful examination which has been made of the three officials with whom these communications took place, that none of them used any improper means of approaching the prisoners, and that the statement above reported by your Grace to have been made by Thomas Casey is absolutely false.

"His Excellency feels as strongly as your Grace can the calamity which would be involved if innocent men were punished for an offence which they had not committed, but, after the fullest inquiry of which the case admits, he has arrived at a clear conclusion that the verdict and the sentence were right and just.

"I have the honour to be,
"My Lord Archbishop,
"Your Grace's obedient servant,
"R. G. C. HAMILTON.

"His Grace the Most Rev. Archbishop
"John M'Evilly, D.D., Ballinrobe."

The following is the memorandum referred to in the above communication:—

"Attention having been called in the House of Commons, on the 11th instant, to certain statements alleged to have been made by Thomas Casey (one of the murderers of the Joyce family at Maamtrasna on the 17th August, 1882), who was accepted as an approver on the trials of the persons convicted of that crime, the Marquis of Hartington stated that if those statements were vouched for by the dignitary of the Roman Catholic Church (the Archbishop of Tuam), before whom they were stated to have been made, and were formally brought before the Government, they would receive their careful consideration. Since then the Archbishop has brought before his Excellency the statements made by Thomas Casey, and his Excellency has carefully considered those statements, and, at the same time, reviewed all the facts connected with the murders, and the trials arising out of them, and has called for and obtained the fullest information in reference to the statements so made, and the character and conduct of Thomas Casey.

"In adopting this course his Excellency has made the fullest inquiry which the circumstances of the case admit of. The allegations submitted by the Archbishop consist of two parts—(1) That the evidence given by Thomas Casey at the trial was false, and (2) that undue pressure had been put upon him to give evidence.

"As regards (1) the only method by which this can be tested is by comparing the retractation now made with the opposing statements previously sworn to, and with the other evidence in the case of the only witnesses who had cognisance of the facts, and who were as much witness-in-chief to the crime as the informers themselves. No other conceivable description of inquiry could elicit whether the falsehoods which Thos. Casey tells are in his present or in his former statements, which are directly contradictory of each other, with relation to the same facts. This comparison has been made with the utmost care, and its results are given in this memorandum.

"As regards (2) a careful examination has been made of all the officials of the Crown with whom Thomas Casey was in communication respecting his evidence, and the results of this examination are also given in this memorandum.

"But, to make the case clear, it is also necessary to state, as succinctly and clearly as possible, the circumstances of the murder, the proceedings at the trial, and the other facts of the case.

"The murders in question were committed on the night of Thursday, the 17th, or morning of Friday, the 18th August, 1882, at Maamtrasna, in the County of Galway. Early on the morning of the latter day a man named John Collins, having gone to the house of Joyce, found the door off its hinges, and on entering, John Joyce, his mother, his wife, and his daughter were found murdered, and his sons, Michael and Patrick, seriously wounded, the latter of whom, however, subsequently recovered. John Joyce was lying on the kitchen floor, with two revolver bullet-wounds in his side, and a deep cut on his head. His wife was dead in bed, with several bullet wounds. His daughter was dead in bed, with her skull broken. His mother was also lying dead. His son, Michael Joyce, was alive, but with bullet wounds in his neck and stomach, from the effects of which he afterwards died.

"On the night of the following day (Saturday), or early morning of Sunday, ten persons were arrested by the police on the charge of having been parties to the commission of the murders. Their names were—

        Anthony Philbin,
        Thomas Casey,
        Martin Joyce,
        Myles Joyce,
        Patrick Joyce, } father and son, of
        Tom Joyce, } Cappanacreeha,
        Patrick Casey,
        John Casey,
        Patrick Joyce, of Shanvallycahill; and
        Michael Casey.

"These ten men were arrested in consequence of information furnished to the police by three men living in the locality, who detailed in the fullest and clearest manner the circumstances connected with the murder, and two of whom identified the entire ten arrested, including Myles Joyce, as being the persons forming the party who were concerned in the murder. The third identified nine of the party, including Myles Joyce, and stated there was a tenth man, whom, however, he did not know.

"The circumstances of the murder as described by these three witnesses will be stated later on, when the proceedings of the trial are detailed; but it is well to mention here that the three witnesses referred to were—

"(1). Persons of unimpeached character, having no connection of any kind with the murder.

"(2). Two of them were the first cousins of John Joyce, the murdered man, and the third was also his cousin. The three stood in the same degree of relationship to Myles Joyce (now alleged to be innocent). The three lived close to Myles Joyce, and within a few hundred yards of his house, and had known him all their lives. They had also known all their lives the five men who pleaded guilty at the trial, and whose sentences were subsequently commuted to penal servitude for life, and four of whom are now alleged to be innocent.

"(3). On the night of the murder they followed the murderers over two miles, as the party moved towards John Joyce's house, and up to its very door, keeping them constantly in view, and were close to them on several occasions, and had full opportunities of identifying the persons composing the party.

"(4). Those witnesses have never wavered in their evidence, or in the identification of the persons composing the party. They were examined at the several trials and cross-examined by counsel for the prisoners, and nothing was suggested against their characters.

"The ten persons I have named, having been arrested almost immediately after the murder, were brought before the magistrates, and, on the evidence of the three persons referred to, committed for trial at the ensuing Galway Assizes.

"Subsequently, in pursuance of the provisions of the Prevention of Crimes Act, the trial was changed to Dublin, and the trials took place in the following month of November before Mr. Justice (now Lord Justice) Barry and special jurors of the city and county of Dublin.

"At these trials Anthony Joyce, John Joyce, and Patk. Joyce, the three persons referred to, were examined, and proved as follows :—

"Anthony Joyce lived at a place called Cappanacreeha, somewhat more than two miles from Maamtrasna. Late on the night of the murder he heard his dogs barking, and looking out saw six persons approaching in the direction of the house along the road which runs close to it, but whom he could not recognise then in the distance. Thinking it an unusual occurence, he came out from his house, and making a short cut came behind a wall skirting the road along which the party was passing, and from there saw the party passing quite close, and recognised as the persons composing it Anthony Philbin, Thomas Casey, Martin Joyce, Myles Joyce, Patrick Joyce, and Thomas Joyce. The last four named he had known, as he himself described it, from the time he grew up.

"As the party passed on Anthony Joyce made a detour to avoid being seen, and came on to his brother's house, into which he went and aroused is brother and his brother's son Patrick, who immediately came out. The suspicions of the three being aroused, they followed after the party of six, who proceeded on to the house of Michael Casey (one of the prisoners), into which they went. After a short time they came out, and with them also came four others, viz:—Michael Casey, John Casey, Patrick Casey, and Patrick Joyce, of Shanvallycahill, the last two of whom were subsequently executed.

"Mary Joyce, daughter of John Joyce, was next examined, and proved distinctly that on the night of the murder her uncle Anthony came to her father's house when they were all in bed and roused him, that he said there were parties on the road, and that her father and brother got up, and they and Anthony all went out and did not return until about break of day.

"No attempt was made to shake her evidence, which left no doubt whatever as to the fact of the Joyces having been out at the time, and under the circumstances described by them.

"The ten then proceeded on towards John Joyce's house, at Maamtrasna, and in so doing passed within a few yards of the three Joyces, who were behind a bush, and from there Anthony Joyce and John Joyce saw and identified the ten persons forming the party. Patrick Joyce saw and identified nine of them, and saw the remaining man (Philbin) whom he did not know. When they passed, the three Joyces followed after them, and in their evidence described minutely the route taken.

"When the party arrived at John Joyce's house they proceeded into the yard and up to the door, which was broken in by some of them, and the three Joyces, who remained close by, heard immediately afterwards screaming and screeching and noises from inside, where the dreadful tragedy was being enacted.

"From the evidence of Patrick Joyce it appeared that some of the party entered the house and that some remained outside, but he was not able to distinguish who went in and who remained out.

" All three witnesses proved distinctly that the entire party entered the yard in front of the house.

" Previous to the trials coming on, two of the prisoners, viz :—Anthony Philbin and his brother-in-law, Thomas Casey, volunteered to give information, and asked to be accepted as witnesses on behalf of the Crown. In the hope that by so doing the origin of the murder and its motive and the persons by whom it was plotted and directed might be discovered, the Crown accepted the two men as approvers, and they were examined at the trial. Their evidence coincided fully with the evidence of the three Joyces as to who the persons were composing the party and as to the movements of the murderers on the night in question.

" Philbin further stated that he saw Patrick Joyce, of Shanvallycahill, Patrick Casey, and Myles Joyce entering the house after the door was broken in. Thomas Casey, the other informer, stated that as the party proceeded along after leaving Michael Casey's house they were joined by the two strange men, named Nee and Kelly, who walked in front, and that the persons who entered the house after the door was broken in were the three named by Philbin, and also the two strange men, Nee and Kelly, and that he (Casey) was not one of the persons who entered.

" Patrick Joyce, of Shanvallycahill, was the first person tried, and on the evidence I have detailed the jury convicted him, and he was sentenced to death. He protested before being sentenced that he was not guilty.

" Patrick Casey was the next person tried, and he also was convicted and sentenced to death. Before being sentenced he protested he had nothing to do with the murder.

" Myles Joyce was the third person tried, and was also convicted and sentenced to death. Before being sentenced he also protested his innocence.

" Michael Casey was the next person put on trial, but before the trial concluded his leading counsel applied to the court for permission on his behalf, and on behalf of the four prisoners remaining untried, to withdraw their pleas of " not guilty," and to plead guilty; and permission having been given, the five prisoners severally pleaded guilty. After so pleading, their counsel in open court appealed to the Attorney-General for the merciful consideration of the Crown.

" Patrick Joyce, of Shanvallycahill, Patrick Casey, and Myles Joyce were subsequently executed on the 15th December, 1882, in Galway Jail, for the crime for which they had been convicted. His Excellency commuted the sentence of death passed on the five others to penal servitude for life.

" It is now alleged that Myles Joyce, who was convicted on the clear and convincing evidence I have detailed, was innocent of the murder, and that four of the remaining prisoners against whom the evidence was the same, and who themselves pleaded guilty to the charge, were likewise innocent, and this contention is attempted to be supported by the statements already referred to as having been lately made by Thomas Casey, the approver. These statements are that his evidence at the trial was false, and that Myles Joyce was innocent; that he had offered to give evidence against the guilty parties, but was told unless he swore against Myles Joyce, though innocent, he would be hanged: That he got twenty minutes to deliberate, and that under this compulsion he swore falsely against him, and also swore falsely against four of the men now suffering penal servitude, and who themselves pleaded guilty at the trial, and, furthermore, that his brother-in-law, Philbin, who was identified by the three Joyces, and who was himself the first to become an informer and admit his participation in the crime, is also innocent, and was not there at all; and it is further alleged that Philbin has made a similar statement as to his evidence having been improperly obtained from him.

" Having regard to the gravity of the charges so made, it becomes necesssary most carefully to review the evidence in the case, and all the facts connected with it, and also the circumstances under which the evidence of

Casey and Philbin was originally given and accepted, and the circumstances under which their present statements have been made, with the view of seeing whether any grounds exist for doubting the correctness of the verdicts arrived at, and also whether there is any foundation for the charges made against the Crown officials referred to.

"The case was not one resting wholly or mainly on the evidence of the informers Casey and Philbin. The evidence of three witnesses of unblemished character proved conclusively the guilt of Myles Joyce and the nine others, or did the case rest merely on circumstantial evidence. The evidence given proved direct participation in the crime, and was based on the positive identification of the accused, who formed one party engaged in one common object, by three eye-witnesses who knew them well, and whose characters were not impeached. The identification was not one arising from a mere momentary or casual glance at the persons identified. The three Joyces followed the murderers for a space of upwards of two miles, and were close to them several times. Neither was it an identification taking place after a lapse of time. On the day next after the murders the witnesses gave the names of the ten persons and description of the circumstances connected with the murders, from which they never varied.

"There is no conceivable reason or motive on the part of the Crown, or any of its officials, nor has any been suggested, why Myles Joyce or any of the others (if innocent) would have been singled out and an effort made to convict them. They were arrested and prosecuted on the one ground—that the information given by the three Joyces was fully believed, and left no doubt as to the guilt of the ten.

"As against evidence of the character given by the Joyces, and which was not in any manner shaken by the cross-examination to which they were subjected, his Excellency cannot give credence or attach the slightest weight to statements of persons such as Casey and Philbin, who, after the interval which has elapsed, now say that they perjured themselves at the trial.

"These two persons, Casey and Philbin, some time after the trials, went back to reside at their own houses, close to the Maamtrasna district, and on returning, as there was a strong feeling against them as informers, they received police protection. His Excellency finds from the reports furnished by the constabulary, that constant efforts were made by Casey's wife, who is Philbin's sister, to induce Casey to come forward and state that his evidence at the trial was untrue, but these efforts were unsuccessful, until the commencement of the present month, and up to that period neither Casey nor Philbin ever asserted that their evidence was untrue, but on the contrary, adhered to it and re-affirmed it. Furthermore, on the 20th of May last Casey was examined at the investigation held in Ballinrobe on the occasion of the children of the murdered man claiming compensation for their father's murder. He was not examined as a witness for the Crown, but for the claimants. He did not then state that his former evidence was in any respect untrue, and distinctly swore that Philbin (who he now says was innocent) was at the murder.

"Furthermore, on the 25th July, he volunteered a statement to District Inspector Stokes, of the Royal Irish Constabulary, implicating two persons in the murder in addition to the ten originally arrested, and which statement was taken down in writing. It is true that after giving that statement he did attempt to say that Philbin was not at the murder, but when asked as to Myles Joyce he said he was there, but did not go in.

"I come now to the very serious charge which has been made against an official. It is stated that Casey had been induced, under threats of capital punishment, to swear away the life of Myles Joyce; that he offered to give information against the guilty parties; that he was told by the official that unless he swore against Myles Joyce, though innocent, he himself would be hanged; that he got twenty minutes to deliberate, and then, from terror of death, swore as had been suggested to him. There is not the smallest foundation for any one of these statements. Casey was never asked to become a witness or to give evidence. On the 11th November, 1882, being two days previous to the commencement of the trials, he wrote a note to Mr Bolton, Crown Solicitor, as follows :—

"MR. BOLTON,—I want to see you in Kilmainham Prison amediately. I have a little emportant statiment to make to your oner,—I am, your obedient servant,

"THOMAS CASEY.

" I want to see you soon here."

"This note was written by Casey, and handed by him to the governor, with a request that he would have it sent to Mr. Bolton, and it was accordingly transmitted, and until the receipt of it Mr. Bolton had never spoken to the man, nor had he ever seen him except when brought up as a prisoner in court. The Attorney-General at the time was in London, and Mr. Bolton at once consulted the counsel for the prosecution, who directed him to see Casey, and be in a position to report to the Attorney.General on his return what his evidence would be, but to take no statement, and hold out no hope to Casey that he would be accepted as an approver without the Attorney-General's authority. Mr. Bolton thereupon went to the prison, and saw the prisoner, not in his cell, but in the governor's office. The governor was present at this interview, no other persons being there, and it is untrue that Mr. Bolton used any threat to the prisoner, or made any suggestion to him as to what his evidence should be, or in any manner whatever pressed him. Mr. Bolton told him what he had been directed to tell him by the Crown counsel, and Casey then told Mr. Bolton what he had to prove in reference to the murder, which closely corresponded with his subsequent written statement.

"It is to be remembered that this happened on Saturday, the trials being fixed to commence on the following Monday, and that the case was considered by the Crown as being perfectly complete and conclusive against all the prisoners.

"The nature of Casey's evidence having been reported to the Attorney-General, it was determined to accept him as an approver.

"On the following Monday all the prisoners were brought down to Green-street. Immediately on their arrival Casey sent a message to Mr. Bolton by the governor, saying he was anxious to see him. Mr. Bolton thereupon went down to the passage below the court into which the cells open, accompanied by the governor and Mr. Brady, R.M. The governor called Casey out, and Casey was then informed by Mr. Bolton that his evidence would be accepted, provided he told the entire truth, and that as he (Mr. Bolton) had no time to take his statement in writing, Mr. Brady would take it. The governor and Mr. Brady state that nothing further was said by Mr. Bolton, and that he immediately left, as the first trial—that of Patrick Joyce—was commencing. The governor also left as he had to be in court, and Casey remained alone with Mr. Brady, to whom he then and there gave his statement. It was taken down on paper by Mr. Brady from Casey's lips, Mr. Bolton not being present, and when taken down was read over by Mr Brady to Casey, and signed by the latter.

"The statement is as follows : —

STATEMENT OF THOMAS CASEY, OF GLENSAUL, IN THE COUNTY OF MAYO.

"On the day previous to the murder of the Joyces at Maamtrasna, Pat Casey, of Derry, came to my place and told me to go over to Derry the next night, and to bring Anthony Philbin with me. On the night of the murder I went to Philbin's, and met him outside his own house—a little above it. I told him to come with me to Derry, that we were to meet some of the boys, and that Pat Casey told me to bring him. Philbin said we had better go or that we would get wrong over it. Between Martin Joyce's and Myles Joyce's house, we met Myles Joyce, Pat Joyce, of Cappanacreha, and his son Tom. We walked on towards Michael Casey's house, and on the way met Martin

Joyce, who came with us. We went into Michael Casey's house. I went in and the others, but I am not certain if Anthony Philbin went in. In the house I saw Patrick Joyce, of Shanvallycahill, Michael Casey, John Casey, and Pat Casey, all of Derry. We stopped a few minutes in the house, and then we all went out in the direction of Maamtrasna. We went down the boreen after we left Michael Casey's and after some time went into the fields and across the bog. We only went a short distance in the boreen. About a quarter of a mile from Michael Casey's house we were joined by two men, Pat Kelly and Michael Nee. The latter is a pedlar. We all went to John Joyce's house at Maamtrasna. I saw Patrick Joyce, of Shanvallycahill, and Pat Casey, of Derry, and Myles Joyce, of Capanacreha, go up to the door and push it in and I saw Patrick Joyce, of Shanvallycahill, go into the house, and also Kelly and Nee, and then I heard shots and screeches. I stopped at the gable end of the barn on the street. After about ten minutes in the house they came out, and we all went away towards home the way we had come. Those that went into the house that night got a light in it. I had a revolver nearly two years ago. It was left me by Michael Nee to keep for him until he would come by again. I gave it to him the next time he came to my house. I have not had a revolver since.

"(Signed),
"THOMAS CASEY."

(Present—Signed, A. Newton Brady, R.M.)

"Now it is to be observed that, according to the report which has appeared in the public papers of Casey's present statement, he alleges that at the interview which occurred on the morning of the trial, and at which he states Mr. Brady and the governor were present, Mr. Bolton told him he was getting a chance of saving his neck from the gallows, that he would give him twenty minutes to say yes or no, and if he did not say yes he would be the fourth man put on trial, and would surely be hanged. That he (Casey) said nothing for about ten minutes, and that Mr. Bolton then brought him to another room, where they were alone, and that then, after further threats on Mr. Bolton's part, he (Casey) started to give his evidence? Mr. Bolton, Mr. Brady, and the governor all state that there is not a particle of truth in this statement; that Mr. Bolton said nothing except what has been already mentioned; that he left immediately; that no statement whatever was taken by Mr. Bolton; and that the statement made was taken by Mr. Brady, Mr. Bolton not being present.

"As regards Philbin, there are no grounds either for the assertion that any pressure was put upon him by any Crown official, or evidence extracted from him by any improper means. He was never asked or solicited to give evidence. He himself volunteered to give it, and for that purpose on the 4th November wrote a note in the following terms:—

"Kilmainham Prison, Wednesday.

"SIR—I have a few words of important matter concerning the Maamtrasna murder. Crown Solicitor, tell him only.

(Signed),

"ANTHONY PHILBIN."

This note was forwarded by the governor, in the discharge of his official duty, to the General Prisons Board, and from thence was transmitted on the 6th November to Mr. Bolton, who had never previously spoken to Philbin, and had never seen him (except when brought up a prisoner in court).

After receiving the note, Mr. Bolton, by the directions of the Crown Counsel, went and saw Philbin, and was told by him what evidence he could give, but took no statement. He again saw Philbin on the 9th and 10th

November, and took statements from him on both these days, which statements are as follows:—

(COPY).

"10th November, 1882.

"Statement of Anthony Philbin, of Cappaduff, in the county of Mayo —Thomas Casey, of Gensaul, is married to my sister. About three weeks before the Joyces, of Maamtrasna, were murdered I was talking to him in Glensaul Bog (we were working at turf). I knew he had a revolver, and I asked him where he had it; that it was dangerous to keep it now. He told me he had lent it to his friends in the county of Galway, and if he had a few bullets from Durkan he would soon pay them a visit.

"On the evening the Joyces were murdered I was at Patrick Quinn's wake, at Churchfield, which is about a quarter of a mile from my house. I went home when the night was falling. In a short time after going home I went out to see if there was any trespass on my crops, and at some distance from the house I met Tom Casey. He asked me to go to Derry with him. He said we will meet some of the boys. I went with him—we went across the mountains. After we crossed the river at Cappanacreeha, we saw three men coming down towards us. They joined us after some time. They were Myles Joyce, Patrick Joyce, of Cappanacreeha, and his son, Thomas Joyce. We walked on some distance together towards Derry, and after some distance, Martin Joyce came through the fields, and we all went together to the house of one of the Casey's of Derry. They all went in except myself. I remained outside. They only stopped a short time in when they came out.

"Michael Casey, John Casey, and Patrick Casey, all of Derry, and Patrick Joyce, of Shanvallycahill, came out with them. We then went along from Casey's in the direction of Maamtrasna. After some time we got into a field and crossed some little ditches. I asked Martin Joyce where were they going. He said there is a boy here beyond and any good-looking sheep he sees with the neighbours he puts them to his own use, and we are going to pay him a visit. We went along until we came on the street at Maamtrasna. I did not know it was Maamtrasna at that time. Three of the men, Patrick Joyce, of Shanvallycahill, Pat Casey, of Derry, and Myles Joyce, of Cappanacreeha, broke in the door and went into the house. I was standing outside. I heard screeches, and immediately I heard a shot. The very moment I heard the shot I got frightened, and ran away; and when I was a distance away I heard another shot. I never stopped until I got home.

"While I was there I did not see anyone going into the house but Patrick Joyce, Patrick Casey, and Myles Joyce. I saw a revolver with Patrick Joyce at the house of John Joyce, of Maamtrasna.

"The above is all perfectly true.

"(Signed)

"ANTHONY PHILBIN.

"Present—(Signed) George Bolton."

(COPY).

9th November, 1882.

"I, Anthony Philbin, of Cappaduff, in the county Mayo, state as follows:—

"On the evening, before the Joyces, of Maamtrasna, were murdered, I was at the wake of Patrick Quinn, of Churchfield.

"After nightfall I left the wakehouse to go home; my home is about a quarter of a mile from the wakehouse, the road is through the village of Cappaduff, and there were people going backwards and forwards.

"After I went into my own house, I put my coat on the line, and then went out to look at my crops and see if there was any trespass.

"A short distance from my house I met Thomas Casey, of Glensaul. He asked me would I accompany him to Derry. I said I would, and we went away there. We went through the fields and mountains,

"When we crossed the river some distance at Cappanacrecha we saw three men coming down the field. After some time those three men came on to the road where we were. They are—Myles Joyce, Patrick Joyce, and Patrick's son, and Tom Joyce, but I did not know him at the time.

"We walked on towards Casey's. When we were getting near Casey's, Martin Joyce came to us, and we all went to Casey's house.

"There were others about Casey's house joined us, and we went down under Casey's house. I asked Martin Joyce where were they going. He told me there was a boy there beyond that was taking all the good sheep in the village and putting them to his own use, and that they were going to pay him a visit. We went away towards the place they were going to (I did not know the place).

"When we came on the street, at the house, three men of them threw the door open and went in—that's Patrick Casey, of Derry; Patrick Joyce, of Shanvallycahill; and Myles Joyce, Cappanera. Noise started in the house and I heard a screech, and in an instant I heard a shot. I then heard more screeches and noises. I got frightened, and am frightened yet. I ran as hard as I could until I got home, and I was afraid they would kill myself the next night for leaving them.

    (Signed)   "ANTHONY PHILBIN."
" Present—(Signed) Geo. Bolton."

" Mr. Bolton saw Philbin in the Governor's office, and not in his cell, and is positive that the Governor was present on each occasion. The Governor recollects clearly two of these occasions, but is less precise in his recollection as to the third. He is, however, positive that on no occasion was any threat or inducement of any kind held out to the prisoner, or any pressure put upon him. He was told by Mr. Bolton he should tell the entire truth, and, as the Governor states, appeared most anxious to communicate what he had to tell.

" The Governor further states that Philbin, on the 4th November, and before he saw Mr. Bolton, sent two messages to him (the Governor), and on receipt of the last he was brought to the Governor's office and commenced to make statements to him, but the Governor, not considering it part of his duty to take such a statement, informed Philbin that if he had any statements to make he might communicate with the Crown Solicitor, and would be furnished with paper and ink for the purpose.

" As regards this man Philbin, now alleged to be innocent, it will be thus seen that he was positively identified by Anthony and John Joyce, and that he himself was the first to volunteer evidence and admit his participation in the crime; and there is this further circumstance which should be adverted to in connection with his case—viz., that when Patrick Joyce, of Shanvallycahill (who was afterwards executed, having previously admitted his guilt), was arrested on the night of the 19th, or the morning of the 20th August following the murder, he asked the constable who arrested him, and who knew nothing of Philbin, whether he had heard that Philbin was arrested, adding, "I suppose if he is he will be taken by the Cappaduff men to Ballinrobe," showing that he was conscious of Philbin's participation in the murders.

"The evidence which I have thus detailed completely satisfied his Excellency of the guilt of the three persons convicted. It also satisfied the judge who presided, and the three successive juries who tried them. Five of the remainder of the party, against whom the evidence was the same, pleaded guilty, and the remaining two, who became approvers, admitted their own guilt, and gave evidence, which did no more than coincide with the independent evidence of three untainted witnesses, who proved the guilt of the entire party, with the exception that the two approvers in their evidence particularised which of the party entered the house. Even if it were the case that Myles Joyce was one of those who did not enter, who remained outside, that circumstance could not affect or lessen his responsibility, as each and every member of the party, which on that night went to John Joyce's house, was legally and morally guilty of the murder.

"It is well here to advert to a matter connected with the case which has been more than once made the subject of public comment—viz., that two of the men executed for the murder—namely, Patrick Joyce and Patrick Casey, in the statement made—one two days and the other one day before their execution—asserted the innocence of Myles Joyce. To those statements at the time his Excellency gave all the weight to which they were entitled, and they formed the subject of most anxious consideration, and having done so, his Excellency saw no sufficient reason for acting on such statements as against the clear and conclusive case made upon the trial.

"Neither of those men ventured to say that Myles Joyce was not one of the party, and their entire statements, even if credited, were perfectly consistent with the fact that Myles Joyce, though he might not have been present in the house, striking one of the blows or firing one of the shots which caused the murders, was yet a guilty participator in the common design under which the murder was carried out, he having been traced continuously on the fatal night as one of the party some of whom unquestionably committed the murders.

"Having satisfied himself after the fullest inquiry that the verdicts in the several cases were right, and that the statements of Casey and Philbin now made are wholly unreliable, his Excellency has come to the conclusion that no grounds exist for interfering with the course of the law in respect of the prisoners now undergoing penal servitude.

"(Signed),

"R. G. C. HAMILTON."

23rd August, 1884

www.ingramcontent.com/pod-product-compliance
Lightning Source LLC
Chambersburg PA
CBHW020158170426
43199CB00010B/1099